Instructional Media
in the Learning Process

Hayden R. Smith
San Diego State College

Thomas S. Nagel
San Diego State College

Charles E. Merrill Publishing Company

Columbus, Ohio

A Bell and Howell Company

This book is dedicated to students—interested and bored, awake and asleep, industrious and indolent, patient and impatient, fast and slow, strong and weak, endowed and unendowed—from all of whom we continue to learn so much!

The authors gratefully acknowledge the following for permission to reprint:

"The Cone of Experience" from *Audiovisual Methods in Teaching*, 3rd ed. by Edgar Dale (Hinsdale, Illinois: The Dryden Press, 1969), by permission of the publisher. Copyright © 1969 by The Dryden Press, Inc.

Drawings of "Slide Carrier," "Bart 500 Projector," and "Viewlex" from *Audio Visual Equipment—Self-Instruction Manual* by Stanton C. Oates (Hinsdale, Illinois: The Dryden Press, 1966), by permission of the publisher and the author.

"Sources of Knowledge" by permission of the author, Raymond Denno.

"Circle of Knowledge" from *Audio-Visual Handbook for Teachers*, 2d ed (Trenton: New Jersey Department of Education, 1963), p. 5, by permission of the New Jersey Department of Education.

International Standard Book Number: 0-675-09164-0

Library of Congress Catalog Card Number: 71-173766

2 3 4 5 6 7 8 9—76 75 74 73 72
Printed in the United States of America

Preface

In his book *The Prophet,* Gibran says: "If the teacher is indeed wise he does not bid you enter the house of his wisdom, but rather leads you to the threshold of your own mind." Searles, in a similar vein, in his introduction to *A System for Instruction* states: "I should like to express my gratitude to the host of people; the honest critics and the false friends, the warm hearts and wise minds, the serene and the innocent, who, with human mixtures of concern and scorn, led me screaming and kicking, to the threshold of my own mind."

As teachers of teachers-to-be, many of us share similar feelings with Searles. However, the problem is to bring students to the threshold of their own minds without too much screaming and kicking—and this is the purpose of this book.

This small book attempts to incorporate within it the theory, practice, and mechanics of instructional media and purposely uses a style designed to appeal to the "now" students in teacher education. It is not designed as an in-depth media textbook but merely as an introduction to the subject. It is hoped that its free-wheeling style will appeal to beginning students in elementary and secondary teacher education, that they will get involved, and that they will pursue the subject further.

This brief, concise book, in a low key and down-to-earth style, hits only the high spots of media. It is a sincere effort to "turn students on" about media and not to overwhelm with an encyclopedic approach which inevitably "turns them off!"

The content is sometimes funny, sometimes ridiculous, but it is designed to communicate to students *at their level.* Most of the humor is student humor—sad, bizarre, sometimes unfunny—and does reflect the informal student chit-chat of the college environment. It is designed to be practical without being shallow and contains all of the basic ideas and philosophy of media in the instructional process. While the book includes some mechanics, it attempts to emphasize practical classroom applications and the fundamentals of effective utilization. It deemphasizes the "nuts-and-bolts" approach in favor of basic operating principles which are transferable.

That, because of its style, approach, and content, this book is controversial is already evident. We hope it will "turn students on" and get them really interested in media in such a way as to improve their teaching. To publish is to stick your neck out—and so we have!

So many have contributed to this small book that it is difficult to name all of them. However, we would like to acknowledge the assistance of the following: Wallace Bradley, Glen Fulkerson, Pat Harrison, J. S. Kinder, Dick Sanner, Jim Dayhoff, Kal Erdeky, Joe Renteria, Dave Sharp, and Livia Charlton.

H. R. S.
T. S. N.

Contents

PART 3

Just Plain Laboratory Practice   98

PART 4

Resources   115

PART 1

*How to Teach and Not
or
How Not to Teach
and Think You Are*

What do we mean by instructional media and materials?

Not long ago a prominent local attorney and state senator severely criticized teacher educators because "teachers spend a whole semester learning to thread a motion-picture machine!" A student once asked, "How in the world can you spend an entire semester learning to operate a few simple machines?" A local school superintendent in questioning the offering of an "extension media" course stated: "Since audio-visual is concerned only with machines, teachers can learn to run these things in their classrooms and ought to spend their time more constructively."

The above statements represent not only misinformation, but a total lack of understanding of what is meant by instructional media and materials. To many, the now obsolete term "audio-visual" conjures a darkened room, a screen, a whirring projector, and a movie to entertain kids. That's it—and nothing more. Consider the absurdity of the foregoing statements in the light of this:

> Instructional media and materials are everywhere around us. They are found within the student's total continuum of experience, from the concrete to the abstract, both outside and inside the classroom. They provide means whereby teachers teach (make possible the conditions for learning) and students learn!

If you accept the above statement, then the operation of equipment (the so-called nuts and bolts) is only a small part of the totality called instructional media and materials. Students will bring to this laboratory experience a number of different attitudes. You may feel something like this, "It's all Mickey Mouse, gadgets and gimmicks, and after all, a third grader can run a projector; why do I have to take up my valuable time with this junk?" Or, you may feel this way, "I really just don't know, maybe I can get some ideas that will help, but I'm so busy now. Gosh, all those hours working with some stupid machines!" On the other hand, we hope this might be your attitude, "As a beginning teacher

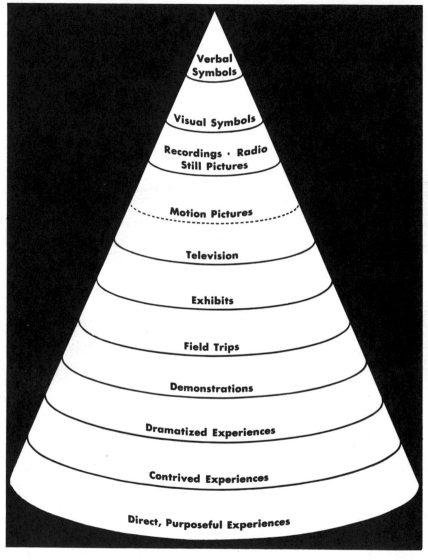

*Cone of Experience**

*From Dale, Edgar, *Audiovisual Methods in Teaching* (3rd ed.) (New York: Holt, Rinehart & Winston, 1969), p. 107.

I need all the help I can get; I heard that some of this stuff can really help my teaching; anyway, I'll give it a try."

Remember, "A chip on the shoulder often comes from too much wood in the head!"

There are two ubiquitous problems, among others, that confront most beginning teachers—*discipline and variety*. Discipline problems just don't happen; they are caused, and your teaching methodology may be to blame. However, problems of control and discipline can be ameliorated by effective instruction—get some variety into your teaching. Variety is the essence of media and materials. Media and materials can provide some of the answers; however, they are not a panacea because so much depends upon the situation, the teacher, her energy, her imagination, and those thirty or more unique personalities called a "class."

As an example of the different approaches that one may use with media and materials, we can cite the following. I know a teacher who is a great collector of gadgets and gimmicks. He brings to class his jeweled oil can, a giant Texas paper clip, a mink-covered beer can opener, a noiseless soup spoon, and even a revolving spaghetti fork. The kids love all this, and he really entertains them. Of course, he gets their attention and interest and may even motivate them. The crucial question is, "How much learning is taking place in terms of the objectives of the instructional situation?" The results will be virtually nil unless the teacher can go beyond the gadget and gimmick phase and get into the real business of learning.

Now suppose the above teacher uses the gadgets to get them interested and then places this definition on the chalkboard:

> The usually red or yellow pome fruit of the family of Malacaae. This includes the quince, the pear, the hawthorne, and sometimes the rose family.

What is it? Students can come up with a variety of answers but are usually confused by the abstract verbiage of a perfectly good Webster definition. The teacher then brings forth a highly polished red and yellow apple—a concrete object that now makes the abstract "apple" understandable. This is one of the tasks of the teacher—to take that which is abstract and make it concrete, teachable, and understandable. This is the role of media and materials—they must be used as genuine *tools* to facilitate the learning process.

Instructional materials and media run the whole gamut of human experience from the very abstract to the very concrete. These experiences can be graphically portrayed in terms of a Cone of Experience (see

Figure 1). The base of the cone represents experiences that are direct, live, and purposeful. As we move up the cone through experiences that are increasingly abstract, we reach the apex and the principle tool of instruction—words—the most difficult teaching tool of all! It is important to recognize that the eleven experiences depicted on the cone are not discrete items, but tend to overlap and integrate with other experiences. Nor are these experiences fixed or final in terms of levels of abstraction or concreteness. A school journey can be the most formalized, miserable, and abstract experience in the hands of an ineffective teacher. On the other hand, an educational film can be a real life experience in the hands of a skillful teacher.

Another way of graphically portraying the media and materials continuum is in terms of a pyramid (see Figure 2). For clarity of understand-

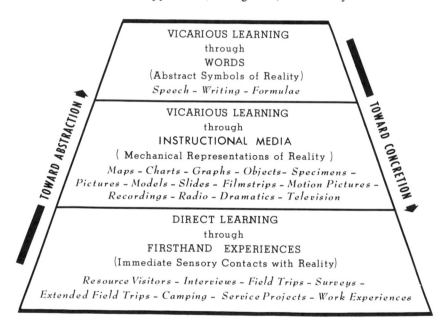

Pyramid of Experience

ing, the pyramid concept may be a more effective device than the more complex Cone of Experience. The pyramid categorizes experience into three levels, moving from the concrete to the abstract. At the base are the real, live, concrete experiences. In the middle are the vicarious experiences available through mechanical representations of reality, the so-called audio and visual approaches. At the top of the pyramid are those vicarious experiences available through the use of abstract symbols—words.

Here is a good example of how the same concept, whether in the form of a cone or a pyramid, can be presented in five different ways without altering the content by using different materials and media. First, we can actually construct the cone on a flannel board using flannel-backed cards and discussing each of the eleven levels as we go along. Second, we can prepare a transparency of the cone for use on the overhead projector. Again, we can develop the cone by covering the material with a card and revealing the levels one at a time. Third, the same material can be displayed on the opaque projector by inserting a book, open to the page which contains the cone onto the platen of the projector. Last, we can prepare a poster or flip-chart of the same material.

Of importance to the teacher in selecting certain materials and media is the answer to this question, "What will do the best job in terms of the teaching situation and the availability of media and materials?" Before this question can be answered, the teacher must have some knowledge of the advantages and disadvantages of the different approaches.

The advantages of the flannel board are that the materials are easy to make and use, are usually inexpensive, can be manipulated, and are amenable to sustained viewing. While the disadvantages are minimal, one has to make a board, prepare the cards, and have some kind of an easel. Oops—they do fall off at the most inopportune times!

Most students would prefer the use of the overhead projector because of its obvious advantages. The teacher faces the audience, attention is focused upon a lighted screen, materials are magnified, the teacher can use a developmental approach (covering part of the material and revealing various parts as they are discussed) and the projector can be used in a lighted room. On the other hand, using the overhead projector involves most of the disadvantages found in projected materials. These disadvantages involve expense and availability of a machine, a screen, sometimes light control, and the special preparation of materials. Also, projected materials are not convenient for sustained viewing—once the teacher flips off the switch, the image is gone!

The flip-chart or poster is usually most popular with teachers because of its various advantages. The materials are usually inexpensive, are available, and teachers can make their own. Like the study displays (bulletin boards), this approach is excellent for sustained viewing. The major disadvantages include preparation time, lack of teacher ability, and display space. Also, some means must be available for displaying the materials (easel, chalk rail, etc.).

Of the four approaches, the least desirable appears to be that of the opaque projector. Not only is it big, bulky, and noisy, but materials must be projected in a *totally darkened room.* However, the tremendous advantage of projecting *opaque* materials, such as, the page of a book, must not be overlooked, Many times teachers are not aware that the opaque projector is an excellent copying device whereby materials can easily be enlarged and traced for display.

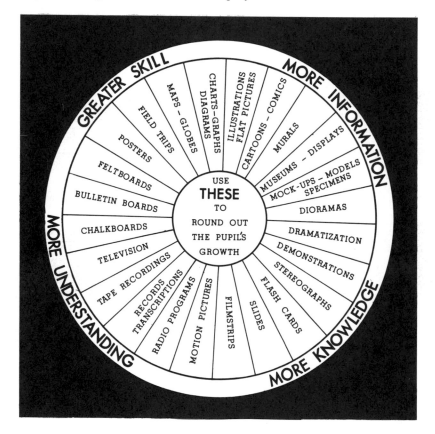

Circle of Knowledge

The senses—pathways to learning

Some wag has called "horse sense"—whatever that is—*stable thinking*. However, we never speak of "people sense," but we refer to the human senses. In learning, there is considerable evidence which seems to prove that the greater the sensory involvement, the more effective and permanent the learning. To establish this relationship, the following survey was tried with several classes of in-service teachers. They were asked to write down three experiences they could never forget and three things they always seemed to forget. Records were kept over a period of two years. Guess what experience the women could never forget? Childbirth! For the men, their richest experience (not always pleasant) was Service connected: sunrise over Tokyo Bay; landing on the beaches of Iwo Jima; and the like. The number one forgetting experience was "names," followed by "losing keys" and "forgetting to fill the gas tank!" Note that what you can never forget usually involves a total sensory experience, and what you continually forget involves a lesser sensory experience. To a politician, names are his stock and trade, and he makes an extra effort to never forget a face or a name. To most of us, most names seem relatively unimportant, and we make little effort to remember them. I'll make a bet—you will never forget the name of the principal who offers you your first teaching contract!

These sensory mechanisms: the eyes, the ears, the nose, the taste buds, and the nerve endings in our skin, are called perceptors and are our continuing contacts with the world of things and events. These tools of perception are the means by which we come to know our external environment. However, the senses are merely data gathering devices which send information to the brain. To make these impressions coherent involves thought, or cognition. Together, the brain's cognitive mechanism and our sensory apparatus provide us with the means of perception.

9

However, it is easy to overlook the facts that we construct our world of things and events through mental processes which are fed data by the senses and that physical objects, as we know them, are the products of our own perceptions.

For a long time now, we have characterized man as possessing five basic senses: sight, sound, taste, smell, and touch, Meanwhile, as we begin to learn more about the human organism, there is considerable evidence that we possess far more sensory apparatus. For example, a number of years ago a television film entitled "Gateways to the Mind," starring Frank Baxter, attempted to identify over twenty senses: fear, balance, well-being, and the like. For our purposes in this book, only the five readily recognizable senses are considered.

Traditionally, the media field was labeled with the misnomer "audio-visual materials of instruction." Since it appeared that over 80 per cent of learning involved the senses of sight and sound, such a label seemed appropriate. Today we know that human learning includes much more than simple eye and ear stimuli. It involves the total organism along with readiness, experience, and feeling to name a few. Thus the term "instructional materials" or "instructional media" considers the tools and techniques of instruction and the sensory apparatus in a much broader context than "audio-visual materials."

Obviously, we learn best, though not as efficiently, by experience—by seeing an object, listening to it, smelling it, tasting it, and touching it. This is also true of an event or happening. While experience may be the best teacher, it is often a hard taskmaster; to learn about fire, just walk through one! Moreover, many firsthand experiences are not available to us (we cannot go to the South Pole or climb Mt. Everest). To short-cut firsthand experience and eliminate some of the dire consequences, society has come up with something called a "school" and a manager of experience called a "teacher." While most schools attempt to provide as many concrete experiences as possible, the bulk of student learning involves vicarious experiences. These latter experiences involve two levels of abstraction: representations of reality (films, slides, pictures, models, television and recordings) and abstract symbols of reality (words). Because representations are closer to the real thing, they are usually more easily understood than abstract symbols which have no direct relationship to reality. Words are merely convenient labels we have given to things, ideas, and concepts in order to develop a verbal and written language of communication. It is logical to assume that those materials which are closely related to reality and appeal directly to the senses are more apt to be understood by students than those materials which are highly abstract symbols of reality. It seems logical to use a variety of media and put some sense into your teaching!

Obviously, the senses of touch, taste, and smell do play an essential part in learning. Of the three, touch (tactile) experiences are more widely used in the classroom. For example, the demonstration technique is the heart of the teaching method in industrial arts, physical education, and homemaking. This is largely a telling, showing, and doing process which involves psychomotor skills. The success of a demonstration is largely dependent upon the teacher's ability to explain and show how something works. However, something which is often overlooked, but crucial to success, is student participation—involvement during or after the demonstration. In your planning, bring the sense of touch into play; let students handle, feel, touch, and manipulate the concrete objects used in the demonstration. Sometimes in relation to touch, the term kinesthetics is used. This involves muscles, tendons, and nerve endings and is best explained by the term "getting the feel of it."

The importance of taste and smell in home economics is self-evident. Here we can often detect the quality of learning experience by a little sniffing and a few nibbles. Sometimes in the science classroom the nose and the tongue are valuable aids to learning. Whether the odors and tastes are good or bad, they can provide valuable learning clues.

REST STOP #1

This *is Higher Education?*

Dear Aavee:

I have filmstrip 1492 scheduled at 8 a.m. on 2/16 in Room 108. Since I will not be there (that 8 o'clock is a killer) have the projectionist show the F.S. to the class—be sure he *reads* the captions to the class—it is such a lovely story.

Signed: Early Bird

Dear Early Bird:

Thank you for your communication of 2/10. Our only projectionist available at that hour is a 6'5" football player. I am sure he will be delighted to show and read "How to Bake Biscuits" to your home economics class.

Signed: J.F.K., Coordinator

Dear Aavee:

My address "Big Aches From Little Corns Grow" to the Chiropodist's Association is scheduled for Los Angeles on Friday next. This means I cannot meet with my Friday class, and I certainly do not want to neglect them. Please schedule three thirty-minute movies on some topic in history for the class. Have the projectionist start the show promptly at nine, and he is to dismiss the class at ten-thirty.

Signed: Conscientious

Dear Conscientious:

Will do—I am sure that anything from our library of over two hundred history films will be appropriate.

Signed: L.B.J., Coordinator

Why do I have to use all of this stuff?

The point is, you don't have to use all of this stuff. You can continue in the tradition of the lovable old 2 x 4 classroom fixture and call yourself a "teacher." The 2 x 4 reference does not refer to your height nor your girth; it refers to those individuals whose teaching methodology is confined to the two covers of a book and the four walls of a classroom! If this is your approach to teaching, you'll soon be as extinct as the dodo bird and more obsolete than the horse and buggy.

In attempting to analyze why you ought to use instructional media and materials in your teaching, it may be helpful to look at what we may call "the process of education." For analysis, we can divide this process into four distinct phases. The first of the phases is the *presentation phase.* Herein the teacher presents information through lecture or demonstration. It may also involve making assignments and an attempt by the teacher to interest or motivate students in the information being presented. Also, the teacher may use a variety of media and materials to expedite and clarify the presentation. Note that this phase is *one way*—teacher led and teacher dominated!

Class tests are the coffins of knowledge. They contain and preserve, but they also conceal. Rare is the textbook that breathes with life, rouses, stimulates, and satisfies.

The second phase is the *reflection phase.* In this phase students reflect upon that which has been presented in the first phase. This may be accomplished through classroom reading, work in the library, or through homework. Again, this phase is *one way;* it is solely student activity, and the teacher *hopes* the student is sufficiently interested and motivated to reflect upon the presentation.

In the third phase, *interaction,* we find the heart of the teaching-learning process. Together the teacher and students interact with that which has been presented and reflected upon. It is *two-way* and builds into the situation the most crucial aspect of communication theory—feedback. It may involve discussion, panels, student reports, and incorporate other media and materials. Through feedback not only does the student indicate his level of understanding, but the teacher receives information as to the effectiveness of his teaching. Both the student and the teacher are learners, and without feedback there is no evidence that learning or effective teaching is taking place. To teach is to communicate effectively, and how can this be accomplished if the teacher has no knowledge that his message is getting across?

Many teachers believe that the *evaluation of students,* the fourth phase, is the most unpleasant part of teaching. It can be an onerous task if one thinks of evaluation only in terms of test scores and the labeling of students with the alphabet soup of ABCDF. The aim of education is learning, and the aim of evaluation ought to be the evaluation of learning and not a technique to separate the "sheep" from the "goats." Of course, the teacher must make some evaluation of student progress, but it must be a *two-way* process to give students immediate knowledge of progress and to inform the teacher as to the effectiveness of his teaching. If evaluation is *one-way,* it is dull, sterile, and unproductive—no wonder most teachers dread the task. Many teachers refuse to recognize the poor quality of their teaching. After all, it is much easier to "put Johnny down" by labeling him a "flunkenstein" than to really teach him something.

Education is a process whereby teachers "teach" and students "learn" through presentation, reflection, interaction, and evaluation. These activities may be integrated into a single class period utilizing a wide variety of media and materials. Interestingly enough, the great strength of programed instruction is that it can incorporate the four phases of the educational process into a single program and can eliminate the 2 x 4 teacher with a tin box page turner!

Certain basic assumptions or premises are integral to understanding why a teacher ought to use materials and media. These assumptions are not stricken in tablets of stone but can serve as helpful guidelines.

    1. *Materials and media are not designed to become a substitute for the effective teacher.* When they do take over the complete job

of instruction, there is a question of whether or not they are being used properly.

2. *Materials and media are not designed to supplant the textbook—* they are designed to supplement the instructional process. The textbook may or may not be the primary tool—something else might be much better.

3. *No device, technique, or material is superior to another per se.* Generally speaking, as far as groups are concerned, they are superior or inferior only in terms of their contributions to learning and in relation to a specific learning situation.

4. *Each device, material, or technique has certain unique contributions that it can make to an instructional situation.* It has certain advantages and disadvantages, and the teacher must be aware of these in order to use it effectively.

5. *Instructional media and materials are not labor-saving devices.* In fact, physically, the teacher may work harder, but the rewards in terms of learning are worth the effort.

During the past fifty years a significant body of research has been accumulated concerning instructional media and materials. In terms of the evidence, the contribution that this area can make to the effectiveness of teaching and learning is irrefutable. Of course there are exceptions, but the generalization is based upon sound empirical evidence. In fact, most teachers agree with the evidence, but apathy, inertia, availability, and finances are often formidable barriers. It is suggested that teachers obtain a copy of "What Research Says to the Teacher—Educational Media" for further study.*

Without risk of over-statement we can put forth these generalizations. Instructional media and materials can:

1. Provide concrete experience
2. Motivate and arouse interest
3. Increase retention
4. Develop continuity of thought
5. Contribute to growth of meaning and vocabulary
6. Provide variety in learning
7. Provide experience not otherwise easily obtained
8. Save instructional time

Media and materials can make you a more effective teacher—why not give them a chance?

please

do not

rewind

after your last showing

---

*Torkelson, Gerald M., "What Research Says to the Teacher—Educational Media" Pamphlet #14, National Education Association, Washington, D.C., 1968.

REST STOP #2
The Art of One-Up-Man-Ship

Dear Aavee:

Please have your Graphic's man make me thirty 2″ x 12″ arrows. Fifteen of the arrows should point to the left and fifteen to the right.

Signed: Pointed

Dear Pointed:

Sorry, the only arrows we make point either "up" or "down!"

Signed: R.M.N., Coordinator

Dear Aavee:

I wish to report some very rude behavior on the part of one of your operators. He strongly objected because I ordered a film for a seven o'clock showing and he had to sit through two and a half hours of my lecture and never got to use the film. I can't understand why he would complain because he was being paid by the hour and besides he must have learned something from my lecture.

Signed: Insulted

Dear Insulted:

The operator has been properly reprimanded. He had the gall to say that you read from a book for the entire two and a half hours. Can you imagine a professor ever doing this? Besides, I think it a compliment when a professor gets so involved with his reading that he forgets to use the film.

Signed: F.D.R., Coordinator

Where do I find instructional media and materials?

Media and materials are everywhere around us—the good teacher is constantly on the lookout for ideas that can be used in the classroom. Both formal and informal sources exist with which the teacher should become acquainted. First, the new teacher should inquire about the sources available within the school and the resource center with which the district is affiliated. If you teach in a large district, most likely it will have its own Instructional Resources Center. However, if the district is small, it may be affiliated with another district or county center. In any event, these centers will have a wide variety of media and materials available for teachers. Also, most centers will include a curriculum library which can be a valuable teacher resource. Usually, instructions on how to order materials along with a variety of media catalogs are available in individual schools.

Most college campuses will have an Audio-Visual Service Center for faculty use. Moreover, some centers will permit students to use materials for their student teaching—check your local campus.

A growing number of college campuses, schools, or departments of education are establishing Instructional Resource Centers. These centers, established primarily for students in education, may include a curriculum materials library, a service center (for equipment and materials), a media laboratory (for equipment operation), and a production laboratory. Depending on the size of the operation, students may learn to operate a variety of equipment and make materials to be used in their teaching. The latter materials may include spirit masters, bulletin boards, flannel boards, dry-mounting, overhead transparencies, and the like.

Most curriculum libraries will contain a wide variety of education periodicals available to teachers. Other sources where students can obtain ideas and materials are the college bookstore, paint and hobby shops, hardware stores, and commercial display stores. Browse through the local bookstore and discover the wide variety of pamphlets, materials, and ideas to enrich your teaching.

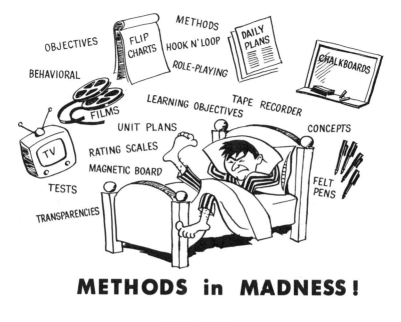

METHODS in MADNESS!

REST STOP #3
Calling All Tapeworms

Dear Aavee:

I have tried to use a tape recorder to tape a program from my radio, and I also tried to duplicate another tape. Each time I received such an electric shock my eyes are still crossed. Besides, the recording was lousy. What did I do wrong?

Signed: Crossed Eyes

Dear Crossed Eyes:

Sometimes it helps to read the instructions that came with your tape recorder. When recording from either the radio or another tape recorder, turn on the monitor and "listen in" to the quality of your recording.

Signed: R. McKuen,
Coordinator

How can I effectively use instructional media and materials?

Effective utilization is the most important aspect of an instructional media experience. Unfortunately, media and materials are used improperly more often than correctly. Think back upon the hundreds of films you have had to sit through during your experiences as a student. How many times did the teacher really prepare for the presentation of the film? Did he really try to get you interested, tell you what to look for, and inform you what was expected? How ready were you, and what kind of follow-up was used to clinch the instructional objectives? More often than not, you remember this, "Well, now that we've seen the movie, let's get down to work!" How often was the film an integral part of the lesson plan? It would be difficult to venture a guess as to the percentage of times films are used to take up time, entertain students, and permit the teacher to sneak out for morning coffee.

Media and materials *must* be used as an integral part of the over-all lesson plan. If they cannot be used in this manner, not only is the teacher wasting student time, but he is guilty of educational quackery. Most students are aware of the basic elements in lesson planning. These are: (1) behavioral objectives (just what is it, in behavioral terms, that *students will be able to do* upon completion of the lesson—identify, classify, compare, discuss?); (2) evaluation (students *are able to do what?*); (3) media and materials (what media and materials will you select in order to achieve the objectives?); (4) activities—teacher (what kinds of activities and techniques involving media and materials will the teacher use to help students achieve the objectives of the lesson?); (5) activities—students (with what kinds of activities will students be involved in order to achieve the lesson objectives?); and (6) post-analysis (How did I do today?—Dear Diary, I sure was great today because . . .). Note that media and materials do not alter the basic elements of the lesson plan; they are an integral part of the over-all planning.

"Turn it off in 45 minutes and dismiss the class."

Many teachers are guilty of what some have called the R.O.G. Syndrome. This means "running out of gas" and is usually the result of poor planning. Using media and materials, especially if they are mechanical in nature, often requires rehearsal and a carefully timed planned performance. Also, he must get the job done before the class is over. Once the bell rings, no matter how interesting the lesson might be, "you've had it!" Most skillful teachers develop some interesting tapering-off techniques.

A word of warning.

If the materials to be presented are mechanical in nature and involve a single sensory approach, as with a tape recording, a film-strip, or a record, the teacher *must* supplement the materials with other stimuli. He should not be surprised when his favorite recording falls flat on its face because he has failed to supplement this audio experience with some visual imagery. With film-strips the teacher must supplement and enrich the visual image with the audio (the voice of the teacher). In other words, if learning in terms of the objectives is to take place, the task of the teacher is to guide the looking and listening. However, he must not overdo it! Too many stimuli can confuse and frustrate the student. A good technique, even with educational films, is to place a series of questions which students ought to be able to answer on the chalkboard upon completion of the presentation.

One of the difficulties often encountered by beginning teachers is "getting down to the level of students." A number of years ago some psychologists came up with what they called the "COIK" fallacy (clear only if known). In other words, you have to start where the students are if learning is to take place. The Marines use a further refinement of this principle which is called "KISS" (keep it simple stupid!). The basic elements in effective media utilization are as simple as "KISS." The initials are PPPF—Prepare yourself; Prepare your students; Present the material under the best possible conditions; and follow up.

Verbalism—funny but sad!

Now that you have been exposed to all this verbiage, let's confuse the issue by bringing in a new term "verbalism." This term is closely related to effective utilization, as well as teacher planning and organization. It represents some of the pedaguese of media specialists. Verbalism is the symptom of a disease usually caught in school—the use of words without understanding. For this often sad but funny paroxysm, the only known antidote is effective and skillful teaching. Verbalizing, the use of words to communicate, is not to be confused with verbalism; the latter may have just the opposite effect. However, inherent in the verbalizing process is this ever-present danger: the use of words without knowledge, comprehension, and understanding thereof.

Because of their humor, often dubious at best, verbalisms are easy to recall:

"The Chinese worshipped their aunt's sisters."
"Lead us not into Penn Station."
"The Equator is a menagerie lion running around the earth."

Closely allied to the verbalism is the malapropism, the misuse or misplacement of a word by accident or intention. Malapropisms may run something like this: A young lady in announcing the purchase of an expensive black dress described it as "black and gold and all covered with Seagrams." Or this from the evaluation report of an Air Force candidate, "He has a very congenital personality."

The verbalism and the malapropism are closely related to learning and may, or may not be, the result of ineffective teaching. The differences between these two "linguistic errors" is that the malapropism may be accidental, intentional, or the result of situational stress and pressure. On the other hand, the verbalism is not intentional and, while it may involve the misuse of a word, it clearly indicates a lack of understanding.

Because media and materials are more concrete than word symbols, they can help prevent the disease of verbalism. Therefore, with media and materials the teacher must first *prepare himself* by adequate planning and organization. In planning, the establishing of objectives comes first, followed by the selection of media, materials, and activities in terms of the objectives. It is essential that the teacher makes a genuine effort to discover all he can about the materials. Preview, if possible, or talk to other teachers, or use the study guide which may accompany the materials. In any event, he must know the content of the materials to determine if they are compatible with the objectives. Believe it or not, after seeing a film on Greece, Johnny went to the librarian and requested the book "The Homeless Idiot." After much probing the librarian discovered he wanted "Homer's Iliad!"

Secondly, for effective utilization the teacher must *prepare the students.* He must get them ready, and they must know what is going on. If the teacher's aim is to have students flunk the test or have a nice normal grading curve—by all means he must keep his plan a deep, dark secret. In all fairness to those precious commodities in our classrooms, they must be informed of the teacher's plan; the objectives to be achieved (often the teacher doesn't know either); why the teacher has chosen these particular materials and activities; and exactly what is expected of students. How can students achieve objectives of the lesson if they have no knowledge of what they are?

How many times have you heard students repeat the Pledge of Allegiance as "one nation invisible" or "one naked individual?" Then there was the student who wanted to know the location of my country "tisofthee!" We all know the words to God Bless America, yet one student sang it like this:

> God bless America, land that I love,
> Stand beside her and guide her,
> With the LIGHT FROM A BULB!

Somewhere, somehow a teacher has failed. Schools by their very nature promote verbalism. Words form the heart of the communication process and most teachers place a disproportionate emphasis on them. Words alone cannot insure learning and in many cases may preclude learning because of their symbolic nature. Enter media and materials to facilitate abstract learning by using that which is real and within the experience of the student.

Thirdly, effective utilization means that the teacher must *present the materials* under the best possible conditions. Take care of the mechanics; they must not interfere with the conditions of learning, and a smooth presentation is a must.

Is humor the chief contribution of verbalism? Perhaps it is funny that one student thought "manual labor was a Chicano" or the "Hindus believe in incarceration," but is this not an indictment against the quality of instruction? When a verbalism occurs it indicates that something has gone wrong. When little Mary comes home and exclaims, "A place of great happiness is a pair of dice," some teacher has failed to do the job.

Finally, to complete this polemic on utilization of media and materials, the teacher must *evaluate* now! The best time to clinch the instructional objectives is now, not tomorrow, or next week—get your students involved.

Teacher, prepare thyself, prepare thy students, present under the best possible conditions, evaluate now—PPPF! "Sweet Sue" (Selection, Utilization, Evaluation) as she is called, soon discovered that she and Joe, a Verbalism major, were totally incompatible. Sue is a simple kind of gal who can be as sweet as a flower or as bitter as a lemon; it all depends on how well the teacher plans. Students must be the focal point of the lesson; the teacher, the media, the materials, supplement the instructional process and make possible the conditions of learning.

Can you stand just one more verbalism? The first grader rushed home from school and exclaimed to her mother, "Mommy, Mommy—we had our first lesson in courtesy today—after you have been properly seduced, you shake hands!"

The audio and visual components
of learning

We tend to emphasize the audio and the visual in learning because they represent the greater part of the stimuli by which we perceive and know our environment. While our perception may be triggered by a single visual stimulus, a cute chick in "hot pants," or a bearded figure strumming a guitar, to make the stimulus coherent is a complex process which involves all aspects of the viewer, both physiological and psychological. Therefore, since sensory perception is not a discrete process, there is some danger in discussing audio and visual as separate entities. However, because there are materials which can uniquely stimulate the ear and eye, a discussion of these may be helpful to the classroom teacher.

The visual

Visual materials may be simply classified as projected or non-projected. Obviously, to project materials requires some apparatus to project the material onto a screen: a motion picture projector, a film-strip-slide projector, overhead projector, or an opaque projector. Note that while most materials must be either transparent or translucent, the opaque projector projects opaque materials. The advantages of projected materials include: magnification, large group showing, and attention getting (forcing attention upon a lighted screen in a darkened room). For most teachers, motion pictures, slides, filmstrips, and overhead transparencies are the basic materials of projection. Use of the opaque projector is declining because of its bulk, inconvenience, and the fact that it must be used in a totally darkened room which may not be available. These materials then have all of the advantages of projection, but each will have its own unique advantages. For example: the motion picture has

27

motion, while with slides you can make your own and pace the lesson, whereas with filmstrips it is sequence and pacing, and with overhead transparencies you can make your own (even printed material) and face the class as you present the material.

Unfortunately, projection has a number of disadvantages. Usually the equipment is expensive, must be scheduled, set-up, and the user must know the mechanics of operation. Add to this the necessity of a screen, the darkened room (which is conducive to somnolescence—wake up!) the acquisition or preparation of materials, and the lack of an individualized approach, and some of the advantages may disappear.

Non-projected materials would then include virtually all of the other materials used in the classroom: display materials, charts, graphs, maps, posters, printed materials, pictures, and the like. The major advantages here are that most of these materials are low in cost, readily available, and amenable to sustained viewing. With projected materials, once you flip the switch, the image is gone. Most of the non-projected materials are available for longer periods of viewing, to let the stuff soak in! Some of the disadvantages of non-projected materials would include: because they are low in cost, they may be disregarded (they don't have the glamor of a "movie"), they have to be changed or replaced frequently, and often storing and filing becomes a problem.

It is easy to over-emphasize the disadvantages of both projected and non-projected materials, and this is exactly what the ineffective teacher does. The effective teacher, while he is aware that using them is no bed of roses, knows the unique contributions they can make to the learning process. Other aspects of the visual components of learning are included throughout this book.

The audio—are you listening?

The radio, the phonograph, and the tape recorder comprise the basic audio equipment for classroom use. In the U. S. the great future predicted for school radio back in the 1920's has never come to pass. In Europe, however, school radio has been widely used, although current use is diminishing. Where instructional materials and equipment are extremely limited, school radio can be used because of availability and low cost. In the U. S., where a variety of materials and equipment are often available to the teacher, school radio has had little success. In fact, the advantages of immediacy (on the spot broadcasts, news, current events) and ease of operation are far outweighed by the problem of scheduling.

On the other hand, the phonograph, which once enjoyed great popularity in the classroom, has some of the advantages of radio (with the exception of immediacy), but eliminates the scheduling problem. However, the storage and deterioration of records remains a problem.

Of the three pieces of audio equipment, the tape recorder appears to be most popular with teachers. It has all of the advantages of radio (except immediacy) and all of the advantages of the phonograph. However, it eliminates some of the disadvantages of both and has some unique advantages of its own. It has high fidelity; the tape does not deteriorate rapidly; it is easy to stop, start, edit, and erase; and the tape can be reused over and over again.

Of the three audio components, all have these common disadvantages: (1) they involve a single sensory approach (one-way communication); (2) the listener must accept the message at the rate it is transmitted (this is a more serious problem with T. V. and films since you can stop and start the phonograph or tape recorder). However, the use of experts, or specialists for radio, records, or tapes can add authenticity and reality to the listening situation.

Because the tape recorder uses a single sensory approach it is far more difficult to use than materials that are multi-sensory in nature. If somehow the teacher can involve other senses and relate them to the material being presented, the chances for learning are enhanced.

Be sure to include in the introduction to the audio presentation the "why" students are supposed to listen. Don't hide your purposes and expect students to listen just because "teacher knows best!" This approach can guide the listener and inform him as to what he must listen for. In fact, the previously suggested "question on board technique" works well with most audio and visual presentations—but, don't overdo it!

Just for fun try this experiment: prepare about fifteen or twenty minutes of your lesson entirely on tape. When the students are seated start the tape recorder without any introduction. Then go to the chalkboard and begin outlining the lesson on the tape. On purpose, leave out parts of the outline; i.e. A, B, C, skip D, then E, F, skip G, and so forth. Also, misspell a few words—but keep busy at the board the entire twenty minutes. Usually some student will come up and tap you on the shoulder to tell you you missed "D" or misspelled "teecher." To embellish the experiment, include on the tape some hammer blows, a whistle, or a horn or two.

Upon completion of the tape will come a most interesting discussion of the barriers that affect listening. What has happened is that the teacher in trying to involve a multi-sensory approach has included the four means of communication at the same time! While the two senses of hearing and sight are involved, i.e. listening to the tape and viewing the material on the chalkboard, students are listening to the spoken word, writing (taking notes) and reading what the teacher has written. Add to this the extraneous noises on the tape of hammer blows, etc., and you have an almost impossible learning situation. After about five to eight minutes of this overdose, most students will give up completely frustrated. This is an excellent example of the barriers that can forestall effective listening.

Another technique with the tape recorder is dramatization or simulation. I once observed an excellent social studies presentation concerned with the Louisiana Purchase. One group of students prepared their own newspaper—"This day April 30, 1803"—and attempted to report the events and happenings of the day. It contained reports and interviews with Jefferson, Monroe, and other government officials in both Washington and New Orleans, and with important citizens. Another group prepared a "You Are There" radio broadcast on the tape recorder. Reporters were heard from eight different U. S. cities along with interviews of prominent officials. It was fun, and it was learning.

The tape recorder can be used to excerpt dramatic recordings or speeches from radio or from records. Through highly trained artists, great literature, poetry, and speeches can be made to live again in the classroom. The advantage is that the teacher only need use an excerpt from the presentation, stop the recorder, and then lead the discussion or explain certain passages. This breaks the often deadening monotony of the single sensory approach.

The uses of tape recordings are varied and only limited by the imagination of the teacher. Most students are acquainted with the foreign language laboratory. However, the individual tape recorder can become a laboratory in miniature. In one school without a language laboratory, the teacher has students scheduled individually during study hall to go to a special room and read selections into a tape recorder to practice correct pronunciation. In another school, the teacher uses a two-track system recorder; the student can first listen to a native speaker, repeat what has been said, and then through play back, check his pronunciation with that of the expert. Also, you can have two students record a foreign language conversation of some incident on tape, a meeting on the street, buying clothes, etc. Later, the recording can be played in class for translation and discussion.

If the teacher prepares his own slides for class presentation, he can put the narration on tape using relevant background music from the radio or hi-fi; the results are often surprising. Give students the opportunity to hear themselves on tape and analyze their own speaking patterns and let them suggest ways to use the tape recorder. A small portable tape recorder can be used by students to interview prominent members of the local community. These then can be played back in class for discussion. Also recordings of election speeches can lead to a very lively political discussion.

It is unfortunate that too much emphasis is placed upon the spoken word in the classroom. Moreover, most of these words are spoken by the teacher, and instruction becomes a one-way monologue. Since this is what is, not what should be, somehow we must improve the listening skills of students, and audio media can point the way.

Why Johnny can't listen

Unfortunately, words spoken by either student or teacher represent the principal means of classroom communication. This can cause problems because of the highly abstract nature of word symbols. Through speech we send messages and through listening we receive messages, and to augment this process, three basic pieces of equipment are available to the classroom teacher: the radio, the phonograph, and the tape recorder. The use of any of the above involves a very special, but often neglected, skill—listening. Too often teachers confuse hearing—something we are born with—with listening—a learned skill. We hear sounds, but when we distinguish between them or try to comprehend their meaning, we are listening.

The subject of listening has had a long and varied history in the cultural development of mankind. Long before man learned to communicate his thoughts in written form, whether in ideograph or alphabet, he communicated them orally. Even today, people of the Orient rely more on the retention of large bodies of knowledge by repetition and memorization of the spoken word than do the people of the Occident. From the literature of the blind Homer to the millions of our contemporaries who may be hearing a U. N. broadcast, there has been a long tradition of communication through speaking and listening.

Listening has been so familiar to teachers that we have taken for granted that it has been fully developed in our students. It is only within recent years that we have begun to realize that just as students are unable to read, so are they unequipped to grasp meanings, concepts, and appreciation through listening.

Learning to listen is important because it occupies a major part of our waking hours. As far back as 1926 one study pointed out that we spend about 45 per cent of our time in listening; 30 per cent in speaking; 16 per cent in reading; and 9 per cent in writing.

Here is another problem category for teachers: the *Johnny Can't Series*—Why Johnny Can't Listen! Much of the modern emphasis is upon teaching Johnny to recognize and to interpret written symbols. Yet, the environment to which he must respond is made up largely of visual and auditory stimuli. Does it not seem proper to consider the possibility that in the world of tomorrow reading will be a comparatively minor channel whereby one may obtain ideas and directions? The development of new forms of mass media will doubtless increase the preponderance of auditory stimuli.

We must teach students to listen primarily for the purpose of comprehension. How often have teachers had the experience of discovering that although they have tried to be interesting, exciting, or dramatic, students have absorbed only a small fraction of that which was presented? We call this not paying attention—actually it is non-listening.

Take a look at yourself—really how much of what you have heard have you retained? How wise and clever all of us might be if we remembered only a fraction of what we hear. The only certainty about learning is forgetting. Is poor listening part of the answer?

Just what makes the teaching of listening so important? First, listening involves but one sense: auditory. Compare this with the number of visual experiences present in the classroom. This, perhaps, indicates that a somewhat different approach is needed if effective learning is to result. Secondly, with the tremendous development of new means of mass communication, i.e., the telephone, the radio, and television, to know how to listen has become a comparatively highly complex, civilized skill.

In the history of pedagogy, the first method employed by teachers was that of verbal communication—speaking and listening—Plato, Aristotle, and Socrates, to name a few, employed this method. The great early civilizations used primarily word of mouth communication—ancient Egypt and the Greeks with their Golden Age of Pericles (the *Iliad* and the *Odyssey*) being excellent examples of verbal historical narratives. The education of the orator in Rome with Cicero and Quintillian is another example.

With the invention of movable type in the fifteenth century, the range of written communication became limitless. However, sometimes in the classroom this has been accompanied with a superficial emphasis upon the written word. Often instruction can degenerate into sheer formalism with interest only on style, form, meaningless symbols, and textbook teaching with little thought as to real understanding. Just as written communication received a tremendous impetus from the invention of the printing press, oral communication received a similar boost from modern electronics.

To listen effectively, these suggestions may be helpful for students and teachers alike: evaluate your listening habits (are you a poor listener and, if so, why?); always select a good listening post (don't get so far away you can't hear the speaker); force yourself to develop an interest in the topic being presented; try to relate all of your thinking to the subject (do not daydream, go off on a tangent, or mentally debate with the speaker; you may miss important parts of the presentation); try to anticipate what the speaker may say next (this will keep you on the beam); and develop a feeling of urgency (if I don't get it now, I may never have another opportunity.)

The teacher, in developing a unit to improve listening, ought to include: (1) a discussion of the factors which affect listening comprehension; (2) tests which measure progress in listening comprehension; and (3) ample opportunity for students to practice listening. From the above, most experts on listening anticipate these behavioral objectives:

a. Developing in students an awareness of the conditions that adversely affect listening. This includes an analysis of one's own listening and speaking habits, physical surroundings, and knowing when to *tune-in* and when to *tune-out* (how convenient it is to tune-out teachers and parents).

b. Improving the ability of students to detect the speaker's central ideas and organizational patterns. Note: If communication is to take place, it is just as much the responsibility of the sender (speaker) to get his message across as it is for the receiver (listener) to get the message. In any instructional situation "feedback" from receiver (student) to the sender (teacher) to insure comprehension must be an essential part of the planning.

c. Helping students utilize the time of the listening situation more efficiently. Because speech is five times slower than thought, this often leaves a time gap during which the student may fill his mind with everything but the subject. If the student can be taught to constantly review what the speaker has said and try to predict what may be said next, he will be able to use efficiently this time lag between speaking and thinking.

d. Exposing the listener to progressively more difficult listening matter to improve his comprehension.

Learning how to listen is a highly complex but necessary skill. We have neglected the teaching of listening because we have taken for granted that *all* students know how to listen. The audio components of instruction can facilitate the teaching of this skill—use them! ALL the world loves a good listener; are you listening?

REST STOP #4
From the Teacher's Waste Basket

Dear Aavee:

Our Building Coordinator is a wolf, and I'm afraid to go into a dark room with him to learn how to run a projector. Can you help me?

Signed: Frightened

Dear Frightened:

I suggest you take the Instructional Media Extension course and then you can go into the dark room with whomever you choose!

Signed: B. Dylan, Coordinator

Dear Aavee:

I discovered that the fifteen minute film you sent me only had sprocket holes on one side. In order to be helpful I ran it through the projector backwards so now it has sprocket holes on both sides. However, something seems to have happened to the sound. Can you tell me what is wrong?

Signed: Helpful

Dear Helpful:

Really there isn't much wrong; perhaps the projector was defective? In any event you may keep the film. We will no longer have any use for it.

Signed: A. Guthrie, Coordinator

Why am I curious?

Because if you are curious, it means you are interested; if you are interested, you are motivated; if you are motivated, you are ready to learn; and if you are ready to learn, then start teaching yourself kiddo!

Sometimes to get an idea across, a demonstration of how not to do it is more effective than doing it the right way. This is the central idea of an article entitled "You Can Klobber 'Em." * The article demonstrates how a teacher can utilize a film in such a way that one-half of the students are guaranteed "A's" on the follow-up test while the other students are guaranteed failure. Merely by informing one group what to look for and what is expected of them and giving no information to the other group, you can really "klobber 'em!"

The film "Duplicating By the Spirit Method" † can provide a good example of a how not to do it. This film has content that most beginning teachers are interested in. One of the first tasks a student will be given by the master teacher is, "Run this off on the ditto machine." Some students will have had previous experience, but the majority will not know which end to start with. Therefore, it is imperative that student teachers have some knowledge of how to operate the spirit duplicator. If we start the session off with this kind of an introduction, "Today we're going to have a movie, look at it!" we have set the proper tone for the demonstration. Now the fun begins; blast out with the sound, start with the numbers, not the title, have the image way out of focus and spilling off the screen. There are all kinds of things you can do; fiddle with the lens, wiggle your fingers on the screen, kick the projector stand, fall over the cord, walk in front of the projector several times,

---

* Hayden R. Smith, "You Can Klobber 'Em," *Educational Screen and Audio-Visual Guide* (Jan. 1963), pp. 18-19, 27.

† Bailey Films, Hollywood, Calif. 15 mins., color.

play with the zoom lens, the sound, lose the film loops, run it in reverse—anything to frustrate the student and forestall learning. For a perfect ending, finish up with the sound blasting away and let the film run out until that beautiful stark white light appears on the screen. Here is an excellent example of a smooth showing. Don't laugh—it does happen in classrooms and you know it.

"Sorry, Dr. Whitmore, but the A-V budget will only go so far."

Half-way through the performance most students will catch on, but a number will be highly incensed at the stupidity of the instructor and his projectionist. In the follow-up, students will stress the points that they just were not ready and needed a good introduction in terms of what to look for and what was expected of them. Also, they are quickly aware of how the mechanics of projection can easily destroy the teaching effectiveness of a good film. It is interesting that students at the college level, because of their ability and experience, will make a valiant attempt to learn from a film despite all of the barriers placed in front of them. Unfortunately, this is not true in most elementary and secondary classrooms.

Duplicating materials to hand out to students can be a valuable aid to the classroom teacher. Learning to operate a duplicator is a rather simple process and can be learned in a few minutes. Yet, how many teachers have left the protection sheet in as they have typed the master? I have! Spirit duplicators may be operated manually or electrically. All machines will have these basic parts: a fluid tank (which you will have to turn on), a wick (to control the amount of fluid), a pressure control (to control the pressure of the copy on the paper), a clamp (to clamp in the master), a feed control (to control the feed of paper into the machine), tray adjustments (for various sizes of paper), and a switch or hand crank. All machines are slightly different, but they will have the above basic controls. Look for them—practice a little—and away you go.

Besides hand-out materials, there are two aids available in every classroom—sometimes—the chalkboard and the bulletin board. The chalkboard is perhaps the most universal tool used by teachers. Its chief advantage is that it is immediately available for on-the-spot explanation. It is a difficult writing surface and should not be used for reams of written materials. Because of its low contrast and flat surface, it does not lend itself to easy communication. Use a good grade of chalk, write big, and clean with the dry method (a soft chamois) instead of with water. A green board is best because it lessens eye fatigue. These are a few of the ideas contained in the film "Chalk and Chalkboards." *

For teachers there is a great deal of material available concerning the so-called bulletin board (a more appropriate term is "study display"). Browse through the local bookstore, and you will be amazed at the number of pamphlets covering a wide variety of interesting ideas. The chief advantage of the study display is that it is a communication device for the sustained viewing of learning materials. Not only can it be a display for student materials, but by involving students in production it can be a valuable motivating and learning technique. An excellent film to view is "Bulletin Boards: An Effective Teaching Device." †

For convenience and analysis it is possible to look at media and materials in terms of two basic categories: projected materials vs. non-projected materials. The librarians classify this area as being simply either *book* or *non-book,* and naturally you know which is best! Attempting to classify has an inherent danger of over-simplification. However, in classifying media and materials as projected or non-projected you are primarily concerned with instructional techniques.

Non-projected materials may include all printed materials, such as, books, hand-outs, study prints, and teacher-made materials. The latter would include charts, posters, and graphs, along with a wide array of photographic and other graphic materials. The chief advantages of the

---

*Bailey Films, Hollywood, Calif., 15 mins., color.
†Bailey Films, Hollywood, Calif., 15 mins., color.

above materials, with the exception of books, are that they are usually available, low in cost, and amenable to sustained viewing for instructional purposes. On the debit side of the ledger, these materials are bulky and often difficult to store and file, are time-consuming to produce, become worn and frayed, and sometimes are costly.

While non-projected materials are usually opaque in nature, it is possible to project them on the opaque projector. On the other hand, projected materials must be either transparent or translucent. However, the overhead projector can be used for opaque materials (silhouettes, etc.).

"This wasn't what I had in mind when I requested an overhead projector."

Most projected materials are either pictures or graphics, and they may be stills (slides) or have motion (films). If motion is important to the learning objectives, then films are best. It all depends upon the teaching situation. While flat pictures, slides, and films are widely used to facilitate learning, few teachers are aware of both the advantages and disadvantages of these media.

What's this jazz about seeing is not believing?

So glad you asked that one. It means that sometimes we cannot even trust our senses, especially in the visual area. Often what we see, hear, and do is not determined by the situation, but by the experiences we bring to the situation. This involves the fascinating psychological area called perception. Simply, perception or perceiving involves an awareness of the existence of material objects through visual stimuli. However, if effective perceptual learning is to take place it involves not only awareness, but an understanding of the conditions and relationships within the total visual situation. Because of hidden elements within pictures, trick photos, and drawings and the part experience plays in perception, what we see or think we see may not be true, and it may result in misdirected learning. In using visual materials, especially if they are graphic in nature, the principal task of the teacher is to expand the student's superficial glance into a careful scrutiny of the total content.

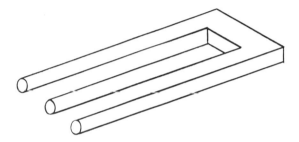

How's Your Perception?

We have often heard this expression, "Confucius say, a picture is worth a thousand words." Not only is such a statement ridiculous in terms of the instructional situation, but Confucius never said such a thing! It was an A.V. buff from Detroit who, in 1918, coined the slogan to sell filmstrips. For desirable learning outcomes, pictures do not speak for themselves, and it may be the words of the skillful teacher that are crucial if learning is to take place. Words should be used by the teacher as clues or cues in terms of the various picture elements. He may point out such items as size, contrast, direction, comparison, figure, and ground and can help students really learn from pictures. In fact, "Words may be worth more than picture!"

Research has revealed that most students look at pictures in the same manner they read the printed page. They usually start at the upper left-hand corner and proceed from left to right. However, students may be satisfied with the first superficial glance and proceed no further. In fact, evidence has shown that more than 14 per cent of the students never look at the lower right-hand corner. Therefore, if the essential content of the picture is located there, they may have missed the meaning entirely. Thus, clueing and cueing becomes the essential task of the teacher.

"Do you suppose we should show these people that A-V Center film on the social evils of cannibalism?"

There is considerable evidence concerning learning and individual differences as they relate to the viewing of pictures. As no two people view an accident in the same way, neither do they view a picture exactly alike. What they perceive is determined by a number of variables: individual differences, culture, subject, experience, and the situation.

We cannot take pictures for granted—alone they may impede the learning process. However, in the hands of the skillful teacher they can make a genuine contribution to learning.

REST STOP #5
Let's Protest About Something!

Dear Aavee:

My darn tape broke—I used scotch tape, glue, and a paper clip—now the machine is broken. What didn't I do good?

Signed: Broken Down

Dear Broken Down:

Never, never do what you dood! Paper clips, scotch tape, and glue are taboo. Splicing is easy if you follow the instructions on the tape box and *use splicing tape..*

Signed: A. Warhol, Coordinator

Dear Aavee:

My boy friend and I had a fight. He says I speak at a rate of 1⅞ to 3¾ I.P.S. I insist that my I.P.S. is either 7½ or 15. Someone told me I.P.S. meant "interpersonal stupidity"—am I right?

Signed: 15 I.P.S.

Dear 15 I.P.S.:

I.P.S. is part of the language of tape recording. It means the *inches per second* that the tape travels across the recording head; the faster the speed the greater the fidelity. One and seven-eighths and 3¾ are used for voice recording. Seven and one-half and 15 are usually used for music.

Signed: A. Ginsberg,
Coordinator

Photography—the gentle art of freezing memories—classroom materials

Seventy to 80 per cent of what we learn comes through the visual sense. Research maintains that the more senses involved the greater the possibilities of learning. Therefore, if they are available, the effective teacher utilizes media and materials that appeal to the senses of sight, sound, touch, taste, and smell. Interestingly enough, some psychologists maintain that there are over twenty different senses, such as, kinesthetic (muscular), static (balance), epicritic (light pressure), photopathic (deep pressure), pain, organic, fear, etc.

Student-made materials involve both the senses of touch and vision. For example, students can make their own world globe by applying pasted strips of newspaper over a large balloon or ball. The globe can then be painted with water colors. For instructional purposes and for drawing the continents, the lines of latitude and longitude must be placed on the globe. An excellent way of making chalk and water color drawings permanent is by spraying them with a clear plastic (Krylon). Not only are the images fixed, but they are actually washable with a damp cloth.

Flannel board materials, because they can be manipulated, also involve the sense of touch. Similar in nature is the magnetic board, which consists of a sheet of galvanized metal, the materials used have small magnets glued to the back. Generally, the magnets adhere more strongly to the metal than do materials on the flannel board.

Similar to the above aids is the hook and loop board. The board material consists of "loops" while on the back of the cards is glued the "hook" material. Not only does this type of board possess the same advantages of the flannel board but, it will hold heavy materials such as a book or even a brick.

Projected materials are concerned primarily with the sense of sight. However, their instructional effectiveness is often augmented by appealing to the sense of hearing, for example, the sound track of a film or a recording to accompany a filmstrip. At present, the most popular of the projected materials appears to be transparencies projected by way of the overhead projector. The following figures are an indication of the increasing popularity of this medium. In 1961 less than 13,000 overhead projectors were in use in the schools; today, it has been estimated that over 300,000 are in use.

Using the overhead projector has all of the advantages of projection. It not only focuses attention on a lighted screen and magnifies but, it has some unique advantages of its own. First and foremost is the advantage of projecting materials in a lighted room and being able to face the audience. Secondly, it can serve as a chalkboard substitute because the teacher can actually write on acetate materials and project them at the same time. Thirdly, because of new advances and the availability of low cost transparency makers, the teacher can easily prepare his own materials. The disadvantages would include expense (projector, screen, transparency film) and the time involved in preparing transparencies.

Motion can be added to transparencies by using polarized light materials. However, many teachers are not aware that the overhead can be an excellent device for projecting translucent and opaque materials. In a science classroom I once observed the life and death struggle of two insects by way of the overhead projector. The teacher merely placed the insects in water in a petri dish and had their struggles projected on the screen.

Most students have heard about the old magic lantern. This projector is similar to those used in the old opera houses around the turn of the century. Herein are the humble beginnings of visual education. This projector uses 3¼″ x 4″ glass lantern slides. The slides are encased in glass because this machine usually has no cooling fan and slides can be damaged. The chief advantage of the glass lantern slide is that it has a large enough working surface to enable students to make their own slides by using special map crayons, inks, and pencils. Available from the Keystone Mfg. Co. is a "Hand Made Lantern Slide Kit" which includes an instruction booklet. This company also manufactures the Keystone Overhead Projector for 3¼″ x 4″ glass slides. Special slides, eight inches in length, may be used to increase the amount of material to be projected. For language development, an attachment called the "tachistoscope" (a lens with a shutter which may be set to flash images at timed intervals—one-tenth to one-hundredth of a second) may be used. This attachment can also be used with the filmstrip projector.

By using a special transparency film, the Polaroid Land camera can also produce a 3¼″ x 4″ slide. Also, the same camera can produce a 2¼″ x 2¼″ slide which is used with the 120 slide projector manufactured by Polaroid. However, making slides by the above method usually requires some kind of copy stand.

Available on many campuses is a course entitled "Photography for Teachers." Teachers should be urged to take such a course for several reasons. Teachers are great travelers, and they will take pictures (everyone does!). Why not get interested in photography and use these travel memories as part of your instruction? There is no longer any mystery about photography; anyone (if you can read the instructions) can make excellent photographs.

No one really knows who invented the camera. Perhaps the early Egyptians and Greeks had some idea of the basic principles. Even Aristotle, it has been said, experimented with the "camera obscura." However, not until the nineteenth century, with the wedding of chemistry and physics, was modern photography born. By devising this mechanical eye called photography, man has been able to study the interior of the human body, observe microscopic insects, view the earth from a satellite in space, and penetrate the cosmic dust which previously hid the heavens from his view. A new development, the "photo-chromic-micro-image" camera can reduce a single page by 50,000 to 1! This means that the entire 1,245 pages of the Bible can be reduced to a single 2 x 2 slide! Moreover, the entire collection of the Library of Congress, consisting of some two hundred and seventy miles of shelves, can be stored on file cards in *six* ordinary file cabinets.

All of the above are merely minor miracles. The major effect of photography on human life is that it has created the most popular hobby of all time. Approximately 50 million people take pictures in the United

States, using 400 different cameras, they shoot some three billion shots a year. Seventy-three thousand drug stores, 160,000 grocery stores, 15,000 photo shops sell film at retail in the United States, and send undeveloped film to 3,000 developers. This is all the more remarkable when you consider the population explosion wherein each newcomer into the world is photographed stark naked on a bear rug at the tender age of three weeks!

Many have contributed to this great invention, Da Vinci, Kepler, Schulze, Niepce, Daguerre, Talbot, Eastman, to name only a few. In the United States, perhaps it is George Eastman and the Eastman Kodak Co. that have made the most contributions to this modern science of "freezing memories." The basic camera is a sort of man-made eye. However, this is an over-simplification because the adaptability of the human eye is almost infinite while the adaptability of the camera and its lens is somewhat limited. Simply, a camera is merely a dark box with a small hole in one end. Light carrying an image passes through the small hole and makes an upside down image on the opposite wall of the box. By placing a sheet of chemically treated paper on the opposite wall the image can be retained (see the film "Pin-Hole Camera" for an excellent class project). The hole in the box compares to the iris of the eye, the opposite wall is like the retina, and the shutter compares to the eyelid. The improvements in this basic box have been tremendous: faster lenses, faster speeds, new films, electric eye, electronic flash, and you can even develop your own color film in the camera in a matter of seconds. Likewise, a tremendous number of accessories are available (one camera has some 287 accessories); one mile away remote control, binocular and three dimensional cameras, and even prescription lens view finders. What the future holds for photography one cannot even hazard a guess.

Cameras may be classified into five basic types: (1) box, Brownie, or folding type; (2) 35mm, 2" x 2", or candid type; (3) 120, 2¼" x 2¼", or reflex type; (4) Polaroid Land or instant photo camera; and (5) speed graphic or press camera.

Of the five types of cameras, the most popular is the box, Brownie, or folding type. Its popularity is due to its simplicity of operation and the fact that it can take either black and white or color photos and slides. Gaining in popularity is the 2" x 2" or 35 mm camera. This is an excellent camera for teachers because of the high quality slides it can produce in both color and black and white. The 120 or 2¼" x 2¼" camera is decreasing in popularity. Its chief advantage, reflex viewing whereby you look down through the top of the camera for composing the picture, has been superseded by improvements in the viewers of

35 mm cameras. The popularity of the Polaroid Land camera is increasing, and the advantages of the instant photo are obvious. On the other hand, the camera is bulky and somewhat messy (all that paper you have to fuss with) in comparison to the convenience and compactness of the 35 mm camera. The speed graphic camera is of the professional type and beyond the reach of most teachers.

Of all the cameras used by amateurs, roughly 60 per cent are of the box or folding type and approximately 30 per cent are of the 35 mm type. The cost of a camera can run anywhere from $10.00 to $1,000.00 with an almost overwhelming choice of size, variety, and gadgets. It depends on how much you want to spend and what you want to do with it. Seventy-five dollars will purchase an excellent camera for most purposes.

Getting the most out of your slides

Whether you plan to use your slides for instructional purposes or just to entertain friends, there are several ways you can get the most out of them. You can use two methods: continuous or occasional. The continuous method uses a commentary to supplement the slides whereas the occasional method may use the slides to supplement the narration. Both methods are excellent depending on the content of the narration and the nature of the slides.

Regardless of the method employed, careful planning, selection, and rehearsal are the ingredients of an effective performance. A continuous slide show with one slide following another without interruption is a difficult undertaking unless your slides are almost wholly pictorial, requiring only a running commentary while your audience studies each picture. Individuals will keep their attention fixed on a picture until their curiosity is exhausted, and for some members of the audience this will take quite a little while. They will follow your commentary only so long as it deals with the picture, and if you wish to depart from a picture and take your audience with you, you must either remove the picture or show a new one. Very few slides will hold an audience for more than 25 seconds or so, and a continuous (and continuously interesting) slide show will require at least 100 slides for a 30- or 40-minute talk.

The slides you select ought to be of a consistent high interest value because, for maximum pictorial effect, the slides must be shown in a darkened room. The darkened room is often conducive to somnulescence despite the most skillful speaker's commentary. It is not easy to keep an audience awake—let alone alert—and a darkened room makes the job even more difficult. With the continuous slide method, change the picture every 25 seconds, even faster if possible. For this reason the so-called automatic projectors using trays of from 40 to 100 slides are preferable to the placing of one slide at a time into a projector. If possible, be your own projectionist in order to control the pace of the presentation.

The occasional slide technique presents less difficulties than the continuous showing. It is much easier to place an occasional slide upon the screen to drive home a particular point in a compelling manner. With the occasional slide, the room should not be completely darkened. Room lighting should be as bright as possible consistent with easy visualization of the slide material. However, in using the occasional slide you may have to use a projectionist and employ some method of visual clues. A remote control device can overcome this disadvantage. Also, some form of light control may be necessary to illuminate different slides. This again may call for additional help. The more help you can get so as not to lose contact with your audience, the better. Flipping switches, closing blinds, and running to the back of the room ought not be the tasks of the chief performer, for obvious reasons.

With the occasional slide technique it is all too easy to address your remarks to the screen instead of the audience. Therefore, the screen must be as close to the speaker as possible. Under no circumstances should the screen be in one corner and the speaker in another. While this might be a more convenient arrangement, the audience will shift its head only just so often and you will soon lose attention either from yourself or the screen. The above is also true with the continuous slide technique, wherein the speaker is at the front of the room and the slides are changed by a remote control device or a projectionist using some cueing signals.

When you use charts, tables, maps, or pictorial slides with specific interest points, a pointer is an extremely useful tool to keep the audience on track and force them to stay with you visually. However, the electrical "optical arrow" pointer is to be preferred to the stick pointer. The electrical pointer requires care in use for it must be held steady, pointed directly to the subject, and turned off immediately when no longer needed. An arrow floating through space might seem funny, but it is a distraction.

The necessity for careful planning, organization, and practice for a visual presentation is obvious. Not only does such a presentation require mechanical preparation, but careful selection and timing. A distinct advantage of teacher-made slides is the personal element. Many times, because of this personal quality, teacher-made materials are superior for instruction than stuffy, impersonal, commercial productions. Students somehow feel that the teacher is making a genuine effort to facilitate learning by contributing his own time, energy, and money. However, a word of caution—don't over do it! Because of your deep involvement with the materials and the availability of a captive audience, you may tend to over-saturate. This is especially true with amateur movies and slides. The rule of thumb is: *always leave them asking for more!* Even when they insist on seeing another tray, or reel, they are only trying to be polite. Most of us have seen so many slides of Europe, of junior taking a bath in the kitchen sink, or Aunt Minnie on the farm, that we have slides of this stuff sticking out of both ears.

Photography, especially in the form of slides, can be a valuable adjunct to your own instructional materials—why not get interested *now?*

REST STOP #6
Of Human Relations?

Dear Aavee:

For my 8 o'clock class your projectionist did not arrive until 8:05. I always insist on punctuality, and your operator must be reprimanded. Even though I did not arrive until 8:25, he should have started the movie promptly at 8!

Signed: Punctual

Dear Punctual:

I am happy to report the operator is no longer a part of our services.

Signed: P. McCartney,
Coordinator

Dear Aavee:

I wish to thank you and your Photographic Dept. for preparing for me the 500 art slides for my Art Methods course. Under no circumstances are my student teachers to use these slides. If they want to be effective teachers, let them make their own slides.

Signed: Arty

Dear Arty:

Beginning teachers are always worrying about improving their teaching. I suppose it is much easier just to use books like most of the professors do.

Signed: J. Lennon, Coordinator

PART 2
The New Technology—Ugh!

Of technology—an introduction

The mere mention of the word "technology" seems to frighten most people. It brings forth visions of whirring gears, flashing lights, neon tubes, and mechanical monsters. Unfortunately many teachers, who ought to be the most informed and enlightened, are often the most frightened. Much of this fear is born of ignorance and lack of understanding. If a teacher can be replaced by a black box, a glass tube, or a mechanical monster—she ought to be replaced. *There is no substitute for the live, effective teacher.* While technology presents no threat to the job of the teacher, it does threaten her traditional role as information giver. Teachers become, instead, facilitators of learning—motivators, guides, and resource persons. Now available are mechanical and electronic resources for storing and retrieving information that far surpass anything the teacher can ever do—and that's what the new technology is all about. Not only can technology help in the storage, retrieval, and management of information, but it can, through careful teacher planning, maximize those conditions which are conducive to student learning.

No clear-cut definition of "educational technology" seems to exist. Some psychologists would maintain it involves a kind of developing "science of learning" where the findings of science (psychological) are applied to classroom learning. For example, programed learning may be representative of this view. Others might view educational technology as the application of the new technological hardware to instruction. However, it must be viewed in a much broader context. Along with teachers, administrators, and staff personnel, it must be conceived as part of the management and operational function of the entire educational enterprise. This function is exemplified by school use of data processing machinery and techniques for scheduling, pupil accounting, grading, classroom construction, and information storage and retrieval processes. Gradually technology *is* making its way into the clasroom, and this is good. As B. F. Skinner suggests, "There is no reason why the schoolroom should be any less mechanized than, for example, the kitchen." However, while this new system, or technology, may help manage classroom instruction, it is of utmost importance that the *teacher manage the system.* Whether teachers like it or not, technology is here and will become an integral part of the education enterprise. Therefore, it behooves teachers to keep an open mind about technology, to get involved, and to make sure it proceeds in desirable directions to the benefit of all mankind. In the hands of misguided zealots—business and industrial designers, administrators, accountability experts, and the like—we can create a Frankenstein. Only the informed, alert teacher can determine whether educational technology will be a bane or a boon to mankind.

Part 2 has been organized to give a broad overview of some of the current developments in technology. It starts with Marshall McLuhan and his "Gutebye to Gutenberg." Interestingly enough, many of those over the age of 30 consider what McLuhan says as gibberish. However, those under 20—children of the electronic generation—dig him—do you? This is followed by a look at the "telly" (educational television), use of both audio and visual cassettes, programed instruction, computer uses in education, the systems approach to teaching, and teaching for mastery.

The linear teacher and the non-linear
McLuhan—gutebye to Gutenberg

Now Hear This:

> We march backwards into the future.
> Man was born with eyelids but no ear lids.
> The classroom—a cell for citters to cit in.
> Step into my parlor said the computer to the specialist.
> The medium is the massage.

The above are typical of the recent writings of Herbert Marshall McLuhan, Canadian Professor of Literature and "the oracle of the new communications." The serious teacher is immediately turned off by such gibberish, garbage, and trash! As one critic exclaimed, "He plays a harmonica, a twelve stringed guitar, cymbals, and a bass drum, all at once—and not very well." Yet, there are many he has turned on, resulting in his being called "The major intellectual influence of our times" and "The most important thinker since Newton, Darwin, Freud, and Pavlov."

Somewhere amidst the satire, the invectives, the adulation, the praises heaped, lies the truth about McLuhan. He does have a message, and it does have relevancy for teachers. However, a casual acquaintance with McLuhan reveals little, for his message is often obscured by his style. For this writer, after struggling through eight books and some forty articles, there is but one conclusion—McLuhan *is* the oracle of the new communications!

The Canadian professor has been criticized as a communicator who cannot communicate and as a writer who cannot write. The eight books and over 150 articles that he has written since 1934 are in direct contradiction to such criticism. A more plausible criticism of McLuhan might be in terms of his writing style. His puns, metaphors, gags, cliches, and wisecracks not only obscure, they often infuriate. What we fail to realize is that McLuhan, as showman, circus performer, and sideshow hawker, is virtually standing truth on its head to get our attention.

Prior to the 1960's McLuhan's writing style is logical, linear, and comparatively easy to read. Suddenly, in the sixties *(The Gutenberg Galaxy, Understanding Media)*, he discovers that the medium (print) is the antithesis of the very message he is sending. Thus his medium disturbs us more than his message, and he is criticized for not delivering his insights in their most practical and lucid form—exactly the opposite of his message. McLuhan's oral writing style (similar to the stream of consciousness writing of James Joyce) is purposive and attempts to create through print the fragmented, disorganized, all-at-once-ness of today's environment. While you may object to the way he writes, he was forced to adorn his message with puns, aphorisms, and neon lights before anyone would listen. In the short span of three years (1964-67) he catapulted to world fame and renown.

Why is McLuhan important to teachers? Of course, any figure who is famous, controversial, and about whom so much has been written, should be of interest to teachers. Yet, it is his message, along with the massage, that must be of immediate concern to us all. The message, while simple, is difficult to grasp because of our linear mode of thinking—the Gutenberg complex. All things, to be understandable, must be linear, logical, organized, and sequential. Modern man lives in a reality which is just the opposite of these. McLuhan maintains that "All media, irrespective of content, do something to us. They massage us consciously or unconsciously—they work us over completely!" With the advances in modern electronics, man now has available to him a total instantaneous communication system similar to his own central nervous system. This new electronic environment is all-at-once, here and now, total, illogical, non-linear, non-fragmented, and often ridiculous and absurd. This is the reality our students live in. The linear postulates of the *Gutenberg Galaxy* and Shakespearean Man are inadequate to meet the needs of our present non-linear reality. The world of print has created a linear cognitive man to the complete neglect of affective man. This sensory deprivation has been most keenly felt by modern youth whose senses are being constantly bombarded and heightened by the electric imagery of T.V., motion pictures, radio, advertising, and photography. Today's youth seek involvement and "happenings"—be it delinquency, sit-ins, riots, pot, L.S.D., Black Power, flower power, or the Peace Corps. They are rediscovering color and sound in their "way out" aural, oral, tactile, and kinesthetic excursions into affective reality.

Students are all-at-once involved in today's world, a rice paddy in Viet Nam, the slaughter in the D.M.Z., the assassination of a president, the riots in Chicago, and even the man on the moon!

Unfortunately for education, theorists can easily forestall reality, but the classroom teacher is closeted with reality all day long. "They are co-prisoners with electronic-age students in a pencil box cell" says McLuhan. He seems to be asking teachers this large question, How can teachers see to it that the necessary specialist sensibilities, inculcated by whatever the form of medium employed, do not become the dominating factor in the entire field of our awareness? Of this he says, "Education must be the civil defense against media fall-out."

Essentially, the effective utilization of our communications technology raises the same value questions as does the intelligent use of all of man's technological creations. Man has the power to use his vast store of technology for good or evil. If students are to make intelligent value judgments, they must be educated in and about the new technology. This is a necessary corollary of raising the right questions and seeking the right answers.

The chief ingredients of education are learners, material which is to be learned, and teachers to facilitate learning. Of this triumvirate the principal ingredient is the learner, because he determines not only what will be learned but how it will be learned. As teachers, not only must we know all of the rules and regulations of this game called "education." but we must also know all we possibly can about our students and the world they live in, not the world we live in.

This whole complicated system of formal education is in business to motivate, to get through to, and to help students learn that which will be of value to them and society now and tomorrow. The principal business of the school is to communicate and facilitate learning, not to grade, label, or baby-sit. Of course the teacher communicates, but often the wrong things; how to cheat, how to forge pop's signature on a report card, how to antagonize teachers, how to avoid work, and how to elude the "fuzz" and "squares."

Teachers are forced to work in a world of modern technological reality. Their students live in the present, the first generation to live in a world in which there was always T.V., jet transportation, and space travel—someday they may live on the moon! They are quite different from their fuddy-duddy teachers who entered the picture just before the electric age was getting up steam.

In the last 50 years many things have happened to all of us, and most of them involve an ignition key, a plug in the wall, or an electric eye to open a supermarket door. The six-year-old of today knows a great deal before he enters that linear cell called the classroom. At a tender age he was patted on the head, planted in front of a glass tube, and told to "shut-up." And there he sat for some 4,000 hours before he met his first teacher. By the time he graduates from high school (he may drop out or be pushed out), he will have clocked some 15,000 hours of cartoons, violence, sex, commercials, and sometimes, something we call "education." The machine-gun bombardment of messages and massages to assure the "right perception" will follow him from the cradle to the grave.

Unfortunately, this is what is, not what should be. The old analogy of the wax tablet walking to school is ludicrous. He enters the hallowed halls of learning already brimming over with information. As he grows, along with others of the electric generation, his standards for relevance are determined not by what he receives in the school, but by what he receives outside the school. And so, it would seem, these precious commodities in our classrooms have one foot in Huxley's *Brave New World* and the other in Queen Victoria's drawing room. We fix their eyes upon the galaxy of Gutenberg while their bodies are being transformed by the electronic phantasmagoria. The gap between the outside world and the classroom, as well as the gap between generations, is no longer a gulf; it is gradually eroding into a chasm.

Learning is something people do for themselves; and people, places, and things can either impede or facilitate the process. The learner comes to the classroom with a vast array of experiences and loosely related facts learned through active, dynamic, sensory involvement and discovery. This is a new kind of learner who calls for a new kind of learning. We try to shape today's students with yesterday's learning theory: schedules, classrooms, memorization, and the like. Conflict is the natural outgrowth when the products of an all-at-once electronic environment are forced into the mold of a one-thing-at-a-time linear classroom environment. The straight-line theory of development—logical and chronological—and the uniformity it dictates are out of tune with the needs of the new learner. The total environment now becomes the great teacher, and if we are not "with it," our students are no longer with us. The current educational innovations represent a sharp break between the linear classroom and its world of print: team teaching, flexible scheduling, no ringing bells, non-graded schools, oral-aural language training, multimedia systems, seminars, research, and individualized instruction. Slowly but surely the responsibility for learning is being shifted from the teacher to the student—where it should be!

The walls of our classrooms and the artificial walls of subject separation have been literally blown out by technology and the knowledge explosion.

The life of the specialist will become even more lonely as teaching, learning, and knowledge move toward wholeness and convergence. However, technology can create monsters and only an educated citizenry, wise in the ways of the message and massage of the media, can determine whether we are to be masters or slaves of the technology we have created.

Unfortunately, much of McLuhan is, as yet, unpalatable for teachers for they are, of all people, the most linear. Young people are more at home than we with the new language. They lack only the ability to articulate and express their views in our language, and why should they have to articulate in *our* language? It is not they who have to communicate to us; we are the ones who must communicate to them!

The boob tube—education by telly

In an article entitled, "The Unfulfilled Promise of ITV" the authors Murphy and Gross, woefully lament the present status of educational television.*

> After more than a decade of intensive effort and the expenditure of hundreds of millions of dollars, instructional television seems to have arrived at a limbo of promise and partial success. Whether measured by the numbers of students affected, by the quality of the product, or by the advancement of learning, televised instruction is still in a rudimentary stage of development. As one of ITV's most indefatigable proponents said recently, "If something happened tomorrow to wipe out all instructional T.V., American schools and colleges would hardly know it was gone." †

Is there really something wrong with educational television or has it finally reached its apogee? Perhaps after two decades of euphoric optimism, overstatement, and extravagant claims, it is now ready to take its rightful place along with the other classroom tools of instruction. No longer will our schools be taken over by station managers who substitute glass tubes for teachers in order to make students into "vidiots." Yes, finally, educational television has grown up, and the errors of the youth can become the wisdom of the adult.

The problems of ETV lend themselves to critical, and even historical, analysis. The history of instructional media is rampant with innovations

---

*The terms "educational television" (ETV) and "instructional television" (ITV) are often used interchangeably. However, ETV usually refers to programs originating from a T.V. station and televised over a wide area. Whereas, ITV usually refers to closed circuit television programs originating with a school, or district.

†Judith Murphy and Ronald Gross, "The Unfulfilled Promise of ITV", *Saturday Review,* (November 19, 1966), pp. 88-89, 103-105.

charging into the educational limelight with trumpets blaring, making a blinding flash, and then quickly disappearing into oblivion. Yet, many of these so-called new fangled ideas did find a place in the classroom and are with us still. School radio presents an excellent example: the great future predicted for school radio back in the 1920's has never come to pass. However, school radio did become an integral part of European education. The reason for European utilization of school radio was an economic one, for radio is an inexpensive medium. However, in America we have had other tools which do the job more adequately and eliminate many of the disadvantages of radio. The most serious drawback to school radio (likewise television) has been the problem of scheduling.

Classroom motion pictures, or better "educational films" also lend themselves to an interesting historical analysis. A number of years ago when motion pictures were first introduced to the classroom, Thomas Edison was purported to have said that motion pictures were the greatest teaching tool ever devised by man and would soon supplant the classroom teacher. Proponents of school radio, of motion picture films, and educational television have all made similar extravagant claims. History, experience, and time have proven the absurdity of such statements.

In 1953, Martin Seifert stated, "Television is a medium of mass communication which far surpasses in effectiveness anything our civilization has yet known." While such a statement is not without truth, it does appear that in terms of the actual classroom experience of the past thirteen years, it must be tempered. Even Edgar Dale writing in 1954 warned, "We must have years of experience with it (television) before we shall see it in perspective and understand its practical capacities and limitations." We have had these years of experience, and we now understand its capacities and limitations. Instructional television is not a panacea nor cure all for the problems or ills of education. It is another in the long line of innovative tools at the disposal of the classroom teacher . . . and a very potent one indeed!

Perhaps, by carefully analyzing instructional television in terms of its weaknesses and strengths, the reasons why "it has arrived at a limbo of promise and partial success" can be discovered. As with educational films, overhead projections, tape recorders, and film strips, television can make a unique contribution to education. Each tool of instruction can be analyzed in terms of its uniqueness, as well as its advantages and disadvantages. However, no particular tool, medium, or material is superior to another per se. Superiority, or inferiority rests in terms of the specific classroom situation and involves not only the teacher and the students, but the subject matter as well. The advantages of E.T.V. are closely akin to those of motion pictures. It not only has the audio and the visual, but it has motion, dramatization, and animation, and it can magnify as well as have color.

Just what are the advantages of educational television?

First, television has *immediacy;* on the spot news broadcasts, presidential inaugurations, political conventions, and the like.

Second, television has *intimacy;* each student has a front row seat, and it appears that the television personality is talking directly to him.

Third, television is a *synthesizer;* not only does it compress time and space and edit reality, but it can utilize, in a single medium, virtually all of the classroom tools of instruction.

Fourth, television is a mass or *large group medium;* no group is too large, and certain subjects lend themselves well to this approach.

Fifth, television is a vehicle for the *specialist* and the *master teacher;* unique skills or knowledge possessed by specialists can be shared by many (often called the D.D.T. or spray-gun approach where you spray the master teacher across the countryside).

Six, television has *flexibility* (within the confines of the studio); with its several cameras and lenses, the close-up, the long, and the medium shots can effectively zoom in on instruction.

Seven, television can *reproduce* itself; through kinescope and videotape, the problem of scheduling has been partially overcome.

Despite these overwhelming advantages, inherent in television are disadvantages which tend to mitigate its effectiveness.

One, television is a *one-way communication* medium; the absence of "feedback" can present serious problems.

Two, television forces the viewer to *accept the program at the rate it is transmitted;* this is the most serious disadvantage of "canned" programs. You cannot stop and start them at will. Added to this is the problem of editing reality and compressing time and space which may result in misconceptions and oversimplification.

Three, television is a *costly medium;* despite the reduction in costs, it is still beyond the reach of many school districts.

Four, television will always present a *scheduling problem;* this was the downfall of school radio. However, if the school invests large sums of money in television, teachers will be *forced* to fit it into their schedules.

Five, television *must* continually upgrade the *quality of its programs;* many stations are operating on a shoestring budget, and their programs show it!

Six, television is designed for the *large group approach;* it is the antithesis of individualized instruction.

As the teacher examines the advantages of educational television, it can readily be seen why she ought to use such a high powered classroom tool. However, when both teachers and administrators examine the disadvantages of ETV, the reasons are apparent why they ought not, or cannot, use this medium fully. Herein lie the reasons for the present impasse in educational television. Costs, scheduling, "canned" instruction, and program quality are serious barriers to effective utilization. On the other hand, the tremendous advantages of television must not be overlooked. Now that the wild-eyed extravagant claims are behind us, teachers can accept television for what it is—an instructional tool—no more, no less. It appears that we have finally come to our senses and at last ETV has taken the right path. This brings to mind a favorite epitaph:

> Friend, as you walk by,
>   As you are now,
> So once was I,
>   As I am now,
> You soon will be,
>   Prepare for death,
> And follow me.

With chalk in hand, one of those bright teenagers of the "beat" generation inscribed:

> To follow you I'm not content,
>   Until I know which way you went!

At last we know "which way television went" and the direction is the right one!

The care and feeding of cassettes

About teaching: life for the teacher is a series of peaks and valleys—hopefully more of the former. Not only do students and teachers change, but the nature of the curriculum and course content undergo tremendous changes. While change brings about problems, the boredom of the same thing day in and day out accrues only to the unimaginative, ineffective teacher. As course content changes, techniques and materials also change. The effective teacher attempts to keep abreast of these new developments—the cassette cartridge is a case in point.

Only a few of today's students really know what a fountain pen is. The demise of this clumsy writing tool was the direct result of the invention of the ball point pen which enabled you to write over butter, under water, and even up-side down! A similar invention, which one authority calls "the ball-point" pen of the seventies, has suddenly burst upon the educational scene and may revolutionize the storage and retrieval of information—the *cassette*. The old reel-type tape recorder will soon be as extinct as the dodo bird and the fountain pen.

This very simple, compact piece of modern technology has all of the potential to precipitate a classroom communication's revolution. Yet, many teachers are unaware and uninformed as to the ramifications of this new means of packaging information. A cassette is a compact package enclosing magnetic tape of varying shapes, sizes, and tracks upon which an audio or visual (or both) message may be recorded, stored, and retrieved through playback. Cassettes have been widely used in business, industry, and the entertainment field. In fact, it has been predicted that in the audio field the phonograph record will soon pass into oblivion. However, it is only recently that the cassette has been making its way into the classroom.

A few definitions regarding cassettes are given below:

Audio cassette. A compact case containing a flexible plastic or paper tape in which a magnetic emulsion (iron oxide combined with other elements) has been deposited. The tape is capable of being magnetized or demagnetized by an external force. By passing through reproducing heads, the magnetic areas are converted into electrical energy, and then converted to sound.

Video cassette. An encapsulation of magnetic tape designed for recording images in the form of invisible electromagnetic charges on its coated surface. During playback, the charges are then converted into audio and visual images which can be observed on a monitor or television set.

Photographic cassette. A compact enclosure of film housing two spools on which film is automatically wound after exposure. Other adaptations of film cassettes can be inserted into adaptable machines for projection, and the magazine load eliminates threading of the projector.

Computer cassette. A container housing wide band frequency response tape capable of great band width. Electromagnetic spots record digital data to be stored or transmitted upon retrieval request.

Medical electronic profile cassette. One of the latest developments is a simple audio cassette available to medical authorities on the basis of need. A complete medical profile of patient data can be transmitted, then stored on a cassette to facilitate rapid access to a patient's medical history. Such procedures expedite medical diagnoses and treatment. This is a good example of how the cassette may be used to facilitate the counseling and guidance function of the teacher. The entire profile and cumulative file of each student may be made readily available in cassette form to the teacher.

For some suggestions on the utilization of tape recordings see the section entitled Are You Listening?—The Audio Components of Instruction.

Utilization of cassette systems

A survey taken in 1967 by the National Education Association of 1,609 American teachers revealed that 53.8 per cent of the teachers queried were using the audio tape recorder in classroom instruction. In addition, another NEA sponsored study of the same year researched educational media on American campuses. This study reported the use of audio tapes incorporated into listening laboratories to be "perhaps the most successful of the audio format of the cassette cartridge." The myriad applications and proven advantages of audio cassettes in formalized education cannot all be reported here. However, a sampling representative of effective instructional applications of this broad technology may be of value.

Progress made in solid state circuitry, miniaturization of components, and efficient, low-cost battery power sources has resulted in a generation of light-weight, functional audio recorders. It has been reported that in excess of 1,500,000 cassette player/recorder units were in use in the United States in 1969. This accounted for about 25 per cent of the 5.5 million tape recorders sold in the U. S. in 1967. Industry sources claim that the sales of open reel recorders has all but leveled off and will probably begin to decline as a consumer item.

The most simple playback unit operates on ordinary flashlight batteries and weighs two and one-half pounds. These units are ample vehicles for listening experiences of all kinds. Since this type of device does not have recorder capabilities, it prevents accidental erasure of recordings. Another version of the audio cassette device is the more popular recorder and playback unit combined into one compact enclosure. These units are providing numerous applications of instruction.

Using audio tapes in distributive education programs can provide students with an effective means of evaluating their own performance in dramatized experiences. Tapes are especially effective in helping to evaluate student teachers in their methods classes, in their teaching of short lessons, and in their classroom performances while on student teaching assignments.

A unique multi-media approach designed for guiding secondary students in developing new insights and understandings on the part of teachers as well as the students, was reported by Ann Martin (1970). This concept stressed interaction between group participants and leaders, and Martin concluded that audio recording of individual responses provides an important record and feedback device for students and teacher. In this way, the participants are able to identify and clarify for themselves concepts involved in their own behavior.

Numerous studies reported programs which incorporated audio cassette tapes in varied areas of business instruction. Butte and DeAnza colleges in northern California individualized instructional programs for three levels of typing and business shorthand by using cassette tapes. Educational Products Company has developed a format for business education programs which permits each student to proceed at his own pace with appropriate interval testing. Obviously, it is a waste of teacher energy and talent to spend 80 per cent of the allotted time in disseminating routine information and general directions. By using tapes to end these routine tasks, the teacher can utilize his time more productively for instruction. General and specific office skills, in addition to business law, medical-dental terminology, and salesmanship tapes, are reported to be available in cassette and dictating/transcribing cartridge formats.

Current literature on the subject of cassettes reveals that they are most versatile. Cassettes are being used to instruct students in remedial programs, programs enriching musical appreciation, classic literature, studies in self-evaluation, and programs relating extensively to all other subject areas. In addition, researchers have reported on the use of audio cassette tapes in home study courses. One authority, Henry Wellman (1970) generalized that cassette tapes have become so practical and adaptable for correspondence courses that they might eventually replace the written exchange between the student and his instructor.

Others have reported that use of the cassette recorder/player, in conjunction with varied other audio-visual materials, results in providing home correspondence students with a highly complete, self-contained kit with which to enrich their home study programs. Other types of instructional cassette tapes are now available to the average person. In fact, Frank Coffee (1970) describes a complete car tune-up program which can be ordered by mail in a cassette tape format.

A forerunner of taped instruction, the language laboratory, is now making the transition to the cassette format. Commercial tapes have been made available for individual study in the carrel or at home. The Norelco Corporation (1970) reported the combination of audio cassettes with color film cassettes to present synchronized picture and sound presentations. In addition, cassette synchronization now makes it possible to pre-record the narration on a cassette player with other such devices as slides, filmstrips, film cartridges, and motion picture film. The pictures may be advanced automatically and in perfect synchronization with the sound by means of an inaudible cue signal recorded on the tape.

An interesting application of cassette tapes was reported at Kendall College in Illinois. Operating on an open policy for innovation, the faculty was invited to try various experiments involving audio-visual media. The most productive of the media experiments utilized the cassette tape recorder. Three members of the faculty used the cassette recorder to orally grade student themes and reported encouraging results. In addition, the faculty reported nearly two dozen new applications of the cassette recorder. Among the new uses were: (1) text-tapes; (2) guided tours; (3) field research; (4) library orientation; (5) counseling; (6) ear training; (7) emergency applications; (8) self-evaluation; (9) capitalizing on current programming; and (10) international tape exchange (see McInnis, 1968, at end of this section).

Like the reel-type tape recorder, the audio cassette system has a number of advantages. However, the cassette improves upon some of the advantages of the old-type recorder. Among the advantages are: (1) low initial cost; (2) ease of operation; (3) portability; (4) simplicity and durability; (5) flexibility; and (6) ease of storage and handling.

The negative features of audio cassette systems include: (1) tonal quality is below that of the reel-to-reel types; (2) nonstandardization of cassettes; (3) jamming; (4) limited number of commercially available titles; (5) not usually amenable to large group presentations; and (6) difficulty in editing.

Other applications of cassette systems

Because of the versatility and flexibility of cassette systems, professional literature contains many reports of varied and interesting applications of this new medium. While many of these applications may be beyond the reach of the classroom teacher, they do provide some insight as to future classroom use.

In a descriptive study of audio cassette utilization, Noel McInnis, (1969b) reported that as early as 1960, newspaper reporters were discovering the cassette recorder's utility. The cassette was found to be of significant help in accurate reporting. In recent months, additional journalistic use has been made of the cassette by professional journals which publish not only in print, but also on tape. These audio publications have rapidly gained favor in professional fields. The cassettes are mailed regularly to subscribers on the same basis as printed material. Some of these audio publications are designed as a method of in-service training or to attain professional advancement. Audio publications maintain the ability to enrich depth of understanding by presenting actual sounds, voices, guest interviews, and sound tracks. In keeping with this concept, audio cassette tapes containing timely documented topics are now available to the social studies classroom. These news tapes come with a comprehensive guide, discussion of the events being analyzed, and are supplemented with dubbings of the speakers involved (Daniel Mattox, 1970).

An additional application of the cassette was a taped interview with Reverend Frank Bates for the audio visual recorded publication, *AV Forum* (1970). Bates discussed the use of cassettes in an audio publication for ministers, *Thesis Theological Cassettes*. According to the interviewee, the utilization of such a concept enables ministers to share the cassette content among themselves, with their congregations, missionaries, and among those unable to attend church services.

Data in a study by Everett Rompf, (1970) suggest to educators considering the implementation of a computer system to carefully analyze the projected costs and carefully weigh alternate choices. Consideration of the audio cassette tape recorder, which could be incorporated into a retrieval system at a great reduction in costs, is suggested. The advantages of cassettes are cited as to initial cost, portability, control features, and standardization of tapes, all of which greatly enhance their utilization as an information retrieval source.

Supporting the above, David Crossman (1970) stresses the investigation of audio cassette systems as possible modes of information retrieval in lieu of expensive electronic installations. He reports information regarding a western college which has contracted for a cassette retrieval program. Because of new developments with high speed cassette duplication equipment, it is now possible for students to request programs from a central storage bank in the remote access system and have them quickly duplicated on a cassette tape.

In a related study (1970), Bruce Goldstein, of Saint Cloud College in Minnesota adopted a total media concept incorporated in a central resource building. Included in the program was a $370,000 electronically controlled random access computer system. Enriching this technically advanced installation was the quick availability of programs adaptable to recording on students' own cassette tape systems. A unique high speed cassette duplicator enabled the students to record desired material. The report indicated that media systems did not have to exist independently of one another, but could provide positive interaction to promote learning.

In the Counselor Education program at San Diego State University, video and audio tape recordings are used in a variety of counseling situations. Each student is now required to purchase his own cassette tape recorder. Not only can students record their own counseling interviews, but they can draw from an extensive library of professional tapes in cassette forms. Is it not possible that in the future each student will be required to buy his own video recording/playback unit?

A report by Gaylen Kelley (1969) considered duplication of audio program materials to cassette format as being an acceptable alternative to more involved random access systems. Citing the advantages of the cassette system, he stressed its low comparable cost to that of expensive computer-controlled systems.

The recent development of electronic video recording (EVR), promises to provide an economic and technological breakthrough in the accessibility of video information. The advent of cassette television has been acclaimed by Edward Kern (1970) "to offer the greatest impact on America's life-style since television itself." Any audio-visual program, either film or video tape, can be compressed into tiny images onto special tape and enclosed in a cassette cartridge that will permit the user to play it back at will. The playback is accommodated by an EVR player and the transmitted image and sound is received and presented by an ordinary home model television monitor. The EVR film is capable of holding as many as 187,200 frames of pictorial information in a relatively small cassette package. This miniaturization makes possible a high concentration of information. The Columbia Broadcasting System believes that, with nearly 200,000 frames available in a single cartridge, it can store the equivalent of a whole library of encyclopedias in a space a little larger than that occupied by a single paperback (CBS, 1970). Cassettes produced commercially are now available to the home owner. These audio-video cassettes will give the user the right to select his own programming, and no longer will he be a victim of mass communication but, rather, he will have the freedom of choice to select what he wishes to view.

An early developer of the EVR, the Columbia Broadcasting System envisions electronic video recording to be an efficient means of achieving better utilization of manpower and equipment. Materials have been produced to aid in the industrial training field and others have been contracted to be produced for government, business, and educational institutions. Combining EVR with other instructional techniques such as role-playing, simulation, games, and multi-media programmed instruction, can accelerate and enrich the learning process.

Marshall McLuhan, the "oracle of the new electronic communications," believes that the information level outside of school is higher than inside and that many young people look upon school as an interruption of their education. Since not all education occurs in the classroom, an increasing number of Americans are turning to home study programs for self education and improvement. With this in mind, proponents of EVR systems believe that this type of recording will make a tremendous impact upon home instruction.

Since 94 per cent of all American homes are equipped with television, this gives added feasibility to the idea of using the best teachers, artists, musicians, and photographers in a combined effort of presentation for home study via television.

Selection of cassette equipment

The audio cassette tape recorder in its portable form has deluged the American market with over 200 models to choose from. Prices range from under $20 to over $100. Teachers interested in buying recorders should be cognizant of certain considerations as to choice and selection of tape devices. In choosing a portable cassette tape recorder, the first limitation on choice is, obviously, the amount of money available. Aside from the initial cost, the purposes and uses of the recorder should be considered. If the designated purpose is to provide individualized study by using prerecorded tapes, inexpensive playback units will be satisfactory. More expensive, versatile recorder/players are recommended if the teacher intends to prepare his own tapes, duplicate tapes, make verbal notes, record material of importance, or utilize the recorder in other ways. Moreover, the ruggedness and dependability of a machine is very important if it is to be handled by several people or openly offered to students. In such circumstances, a top quality model will better meet the requirements for durability.

Consumer Reports ("Cassette Tape Recorder," 1969) considers a primary selection factor to be tone quality. Highly controlled tests were conducted to measure the range of frequency response. Lack of flutter, accuracy of tape speed, and machine hiss were also analyzed in the eighteen tested machines. For purposes of recording voices, *Consumer Reports* reported a wide frequency range to be not as important as in recording music. A desirable feature of cassette recorders to be used in voice reproduction was the automatic recording-level control found in some models. The study cited the feature as being of value in recording conferences, taping several speakers, or in movement while speaking. The report did point out that the automatic control device might be undesirable in music recording.

Other criteria contained in the report included the consideration of battery drain as opposed to using electric current. Such severe battery drain was found in some models that they were considered to be impractical for recording and playing on battery power. This consideration points out the need for careful analysis as to the purpose and intent of the machine's utilization. Operating controls were also judged in addition to features such as storage provision for tapes. Instructional objectives might deem the digital tape counter found on some machines as being highly essential to functional utilization. With this device, specific locations on the tape can be readily found. This feature could be of prime importance in providing ready access to storage retrieval. Some teachers would consider the built-in interlock to prevent accidental erasures of prerecorded material as being of absolute necessity. This feature can be found in almost all cassette machines in addition to being made possible by fittings on the tape cassette enclosures themselves.

In an investigation conducted for the Orange (California) Unified School District, a number of guidelines in the selection of tape cassettes were suggested by Lee Follis (1970). It was recommended that the educational purchaser insist on certain characteristics rarely found in the bargain cassettes: a lubricated sheet lining the bottom of the cassette to reduce friction on the edge of the tape; metal bearing posts or axles at the front corners of the cassette to also aid in reducing tape friction; and a felt pressure pad on a bronze spring to maintain positive contact of the tape on the record/play head.

In addition, it was suggested that the prospective purchaser carefully weigh the implications of the two closure methods of cassettes for his own tape use. Some cassettes are held together by an acoustic welding that makes it impossible for the cassette to be opened. Some manufacturers use small screws to hold the halves together. The purchaser should determine if he will want to open the cassette for tape repair or editing. He should also judge whether an observation window is important to him, or whether a slot will do.

The requirement for the length of tape should also be determined by the purchaser. Standard tapes come in 30-, 60-, 90-, and 120-minute lengths. Unfortunately, the longer tapes are very thin and can wrap up on the capstan damaging themselves and the recorders.

Maintaining the cassette system

One of the advantages of cassette systems (audio) is that its two components, the recorder and cartridge, require very little maintenance. However, some precautions should be taken. It is of the utmost importance to keep the magnetic heads (recording and playback) clean to facilitate performance and prolong the life of the equipment. Cotton applicators, lens paper, or a soft cloth should be used in conjunction with specially prepared solvents produced for cleaning heads of dirt, oxide, or adhesive. In addition, several tape care kits and cassette head cleaning tapes are available on the market at a nominal cost. The cleaning tapes have a feature of ease and convenience since they can be inserted into the recorder and complete their cleaning function in five seconds when the machine is in the "PLAY" mode of operation. One manufacturer of such a device advised the cleaning process to be repeated after every 20 hours of playing time or whenever quality of sound became distorted. The cleaning tape was reported to last for one year under normal use.

Several tape suppliers now offer cassettes with a lifetime guarantee, and if anything goes wrong with the cassette under normal use, it will be replaced. The small extra cost for these cassettes might prove a financial saving in the long run, aside from the benefit of superior service from a better built cassette.

Another desirable maintenance consideration is the nature of the guarantee or warranty. Many low cost models give no guarantee or warranty, and when the recorder breaks down the teacher is left holding the bag. This should be an important purchase consideration.

Most teachers will want a cassette recorder that will operate on AC current with an adaptor (just plug it in the wall), and batteries. Battery operation increases the portability and flexibility of the recorder. However, battery maintenance can sometimes be a problem. Under no circumstances should the teacher use cheap batteries in the machines. These have a very short life, corrode, leak, and can really gum up a machine. Use high quality, long life nickle cadmium batteries which are leak proof. Some models have battery condition indicators which are helpful. In any event, if the recorder is not to be used for a long time, the batteries should be removed from the case; they might leak!

Both recorder and cassettes ought to be stored in a cool, dry place, and some system for the filing and labeling of cassettes should be devised.

Cassettes and the future

When the full range of cassette applications is considered, the future appears limitless. However, because of its almost instant success, future indications of utilization in business, industry, communications, and education can only be surmised. One trend in evidence is the audio adaptation of the cassette as a possible compromise for more expensive, large-scale listening facilities and information retrieval systems. With the increasing difficulties in funding initially expensive systems, more audio cassette utilization in these areas will become increasingly popular and commonplace. Audio cassettes used in conjunction with the up-coming Picture Phone system, hold great promise for expanding and future speculation.

In a futuristic examination as to what the educational image of tomorrow will hold, the concept of independent learning will be in the vanguard. It can be predicted that the formal concepts of education will be enacted in an environment of immense learning materials, unparalleled facilities, and a great variety of human resources and specialists. This centralization of instructional opportunity will come ensconced in the format of "educational parks." This conception, utilizing the foremost in technological media, would provide the most rewarding opportunity for such vital tools as the electronic video recorder.

Just as the tape recorder overcame the rigid scheduling problems of educational radio, it can be predicted that video cassettes will overcome the problem of rigid educational television schedules. While the advent of inexpensive video tape recordings has alleviated some of this problem, the video cassette and recorder—because of simplicity of operation—may eliminate the problem all together. Teachers then can choose their own subject and time for instruction. They would have the option to stop the tape, repeat more difficult sections in slow motion, and distribute cassettes to students to take home for individual study. Using their home-recording video tape systems, the students, in turn, could create their own cassette reports to hand in as homework assignments. In the foreseeable future all households will be plugged into a network of cable television data banks which contain the widest assortment of material available on call. This would include all books and materials in libraries, newspapers and other publications, movies, and a wealth of any desired information presented visually, audibly, and/or in print-out form.

Aside from specific formalized educational practices, many other instructional applications of video cassettes can be expected. However, the largest stumbling block currently is the price of electronic video recording. The widespread home use of cassette television is several years ahead. Moreover, the current cost of cassette tapes indicates the alternate solution of cassette rental. One company has designed a special rental package wherein the customer can mail in old programs and have them erased and replaced with new ones. There are plans for distribution of cassettes by mail, over the counter selling in retail stores, and vending machines; eventually there will be stores devoted exclusively to the sale of cassette cartridges, and they may even be delivered by the milkman!

With the reduction in the cost of production of tapes, the user may be able to build and maintain a complete library of the cassettes. A new process for using vinyl production tape gives promise of reducing the costs of manufacturing. One can foresee the use of cassette cartridges in other areas, such as distribution by stores keyed to whatever products they sell. Travel previews could be distributed by travel agencies, medicine and first aid care in drug stores, and eventually, directions for unpacking and the assembly of products purchased from appliance stores.

Cassettes may be produced for distribution to hospitals, churches, social clubs, entertainment centers, schools, and specialized services for professionals to keep them abreast of developments in their fields.

In the not too distant future no threading of projectors or recorders—just drop it in the slot and let 'er go! Anyway—the cassette is here—the new teacher should get with it!

More on cassettes

Audio Aids for Business Education. Mt. View, Calif.: Educational Products Company, 1969.

AV Forum. vol. 1, no. 3, September 1970.

"Cassette Tape Recorder." *Consumer Reports*, 13:625-28, November 1969.

Coffee, Frank F. "Hot Line Report." *Mechanix Illustrated*, 66:34, December 1970.

CBS Electronic Video Recording. New York. Columbia Broadcasting System, Inc., 1970.

Follis, Lee. "How to Purchase Tape Cassettes." *Educational Product Report*, 3:11-13, February 1970.

Goldstein, Bruce M. "Total Media Dreams Become a Reality at St. Cloud State College." *Audiovisual Instruction*, 15:61-62, October 1970.

Kelly, Gaylen B. "Technological Advances Affecting School Instructional Materials Centers." *Audiovisual Instruction*, 14:42-48, September 1969.

Kern, Edward. "A Good Revolution Goes on Sale." *Life*, 69:47-52, October 16, 1970.

Lewis, Philip. "Schoolmen Will Hear a Lot from Cassettes." *Nation's Schools*, 83:74-76, January 1969.

Martin, Ann M. "An Interactive Media for Student and Teacher Growth." *Audiovisual Instruction*, 15:53-56, April 1970.

Mattox, Daniel V. "Looking at New Literature." *Audiovisual Instruction*, 15:80, September 1970.

McInnis, Noel F. "Cassettes: A Revolution Waiting to Happen." *Educational Screen and Audiovisual Guide*, 12:14, 17-19, 42, March 1969a.

Norelco. *Programmed Individual Presentation System*. New York: North American Phillips Corporation, 1970.

Rompf, Everett. "Electronic Access to AV: Guidelines to Successful Planning." *Audiovisual Instruction*, 14-45-47, September 1970.

Wellman, Henry Q. "Private Home Study Schools and Educational Technology." *Audiovisual Instruction*, 15:20-22, February 1970.

The really new stuff—help!

Historically, educational media have undergone a number of dramatic changes. Early man began the process of change with the development of language and pictures thousands of years ago. However, the most far reaching step for instruction was the invention of printing in the 1500s. This provided some educational opportunity for the masses. During the industrial revolution, audio-visual devices slowly began to find their way into classrooms. In the 1920s, the movement began in earnest and today is a vital adjunct in most curriculums. However, in the 1950s, the technological revolution exploded with the development of programed instruction and research in the educational uses of computers.

As a result of this changing technology and its impact on education, it may be anticipated that future teachers when being interviewed by prospective employers will be asked some rather peculiar questions. New kinds of skills will be greatly in demand, and personnel officers of the future may be asking questions such as the following, "Miss Jones, have you had any experience utilizing the CDC 8900 instructional system?" "Have you studied COBOL or Coursewriter or any other language?" "Are you familiar with current practices in cybernetic guidance and counseling?"

The intent herein is to provide a brief sketch of the current state of the art in two new, but fundamental, aspects of educational technology. Perhaps this discussion can point the way in which educational practices may evolve due to new technology in the next several years.

Programed instruction

Programed Instruction (PI) has been called a Socratic method of teaching, since, like the ancient Greek teacher, it asks of students a series of carefully considered questions. Socrates seldom if ever lectured to his students, rather he asked questions which were carefully sequenced and designed to lead a student from what he already knew to material which was previously unfamiliar to him. If a student did not answer a question in a completely satisfactory manner, Socrates would carefully phrase another question to get the student to "discover" the right track and remediate his problem. Thus, this *ordered sequence* of questions began at the level of the learner and progressed on to unfamiliar material.

A second characteristic of programed instruction is that each question, called a frame, covers very small amounts of material. Broad questions are broken down into smaller ones so that only *short steps* are taken. This produces a situation wherein the learner always has a high probability of answering the item correctly. Thus, it minimizes the possibility of the learner reaching an impasse in the program where a frame is so difficult to answer that he must seek outside help.

The third characteristic of programed instruction is that *reinforcement* is provided for correct responses to frames. A typical program will ask a question and provide a place for the student to supply his answer. After he has responded to the frame he removes a shield, turns a page, or in some other simple manner, exposes the correct response to the item. The student then is able to immediately compare his response to the correct response. The immediate knowledge that his response is correct provides for effective psychological reinforcement.

This method of instruction has several important advantages, the most important of which is *self-pacing.* Since programed instruction is an individualized method, each student is free to work at the pace which is most efficient for his comprehension of the material.

A second advantage is that the *learner is active.* Each frame requires an overt response from the student. Thus, in order to progress through the material, the student must be actively engaged in the activities it prescribes.

Programed instruction can also be an asset because it tends to *reduce anxiety in learning.* Since each student can work at his own pace, there is reduced pressure for keeping up with the class. Also, the embarrassment of failure is greatly reduced when programed materials are used.

The chances of failure are reduced because programed instruction is *validated instruction.* With other methods and materials of instruction, it is seldom necessary for the author to demonstrate that his materials do in fact teach students something. With programed materials this is not the case. When programed materials are written they must be tried out and revised until the author can demonstrate that they effectively teach students what it is claimed they will teach. Unfortunately, most other types of published materials are never validated in terms of student learning.

Immediate feedback on the learning that is taking place is another important advantage of programed instruction. There is a great deal of research to substantiate the idea that the sooner feedback is provided on test questions, the more learning takes place. In using a test as a learning device, it is desirable to be able to provide knowledge of the correct answer to a question immediately after the student has responded to it. The longer the time delay between the student answering the item and receiving feedback consisting of the correct answer, the less new learning which will take place. While programed instruction is not a test, the principle of immediate feedback is used to reinforce learning.

An example of a typical linear program follows. When a student goes through the program he would get an extra sheet of paper to slide down the page, stopping at each set of dotted lines. In this way he would conceal the correct answer to each frame so that he would not accidently glance at it before he had a chance to arrive at his own answer.

Fighting fires

1. There are basically three types of fires. To everyone's astonishment these are called class A, class B, and class ____ fires.

   C Isn't that creative?

2. Each class of fire has some identifying characteristic. For instance a class A fire is one in which the burnable material is wood, paper, mattresses, or anything similar to these. A burning haystack is an example of a class ____ fire.

   A

3. A class B fire is one in which the burnable material is any kind of oil product. A gasoline fire is an example of a class ____ fire.

   B

4. A burning log is an example of a class ____ fire while a fire resulting from some spilled turpentine would be a class ____ fire.

   A and B (in that order)

5. An example of a class A fire would be _____
   _____.

   Did you name something more or less wooden in nature?

6. A class C fire is one caused by an electrical source. An overheated generator which has caught fire would be an example of a class ＿＿ fire.

   C

7. A fire in an oil tank is an example of a class ＿＿ fire while a fire in an electrical switchboard would be a class ＿＿ fire.

   B and C (in that order)

8. An example of a class B fire would be＿＿＿＿＿＿＿＿＿＿＿＿＿＿＿＿＿
   ＿＿＿＿＿＿＿＿＿＿＿＿＿＿＿.

   Did you name something like burning oil?

9. An example of a class C fire would be ＿＿＿＿＿＿＿＿＿＿＿＿＿＿＿＿
   ＿＿＿＿＿＿＿＿＿＿＿＿＿.

   Did you name something caused by an electrical source?

10. Now let's quickly review. Indicate whether the following fires are class A, B, or C.
    Burning oil   ＿＿
    Burning cartons ＿＿
    Burning wiring   ＿＿

    B, A, and C (in that order)

Computers in education

While programed instruction has had a tremendous impact on education, even more sophisticated developments are already underway. We often refer to this age as the nuclear age, while in fact there is another technical achievement which is having a far greater impact on our day to day lives than atomic energy may ever have. It seems to this writer that the times in which we live should really be characterized as the cybernetic age. Electronic computers have had tremendous influence and power in providing necessary capabilities in handling and processing all kinds of data and information in every aspect of our society. Such great reliance is now placed on the capabilities of computers to handle tremendous volumes of information that it would be physically impossible to operate without them. As an example, it has been stated that if banks in the United States were forced to return to the practice of employing people to hand-sort all the checks written so that they could be posted to the proper accounts, it would take every female in the country under the age of forty to handle the task.

Computers have been used in education for as long as they have been employed by most other users in this country. The conventional data processing uses such as payroll and academic record keeping are commonplace, as well as are such specifically educational uses as registration, scheduling, and other routine chores.

Additionally, however, computers are beginning to be used in an increasingly more academic role by schools. One of the first of these uses was in problem solving. Students in mathematics and physics courses used the computer to solve more difficult and tedious problems than it was practical to do without them. This use worked so successfully that problem solving and educational games are now used by many other disciplines at all levels of education.

One of the newer uses of computers has been computer-assisted testing. In most types of testing the problem is to find the dividing line between what one knows and what one doesn't know. To do this, tests have had to ask many questions covering the complete range of difficulty in a subject area. As a result, students have had to answer a great many questions that are either too difficult or too easy. If questions could be ordered on a hierarchy of difficulty and placed in a computer, the computer could then ask these questions in such a manner that it would bracket the highest level of difficulty which the student could just achieve. The advantage of this procedure is that students would have to answer many fewer questions to obtain an accurate evaluation and a great deal of time would be saved.

Another computer use which is actively being researched is in the area of guidance and counseling. Most academic counseling and vocational guidance consists of relatively routine interpretations of data which a computer can be programed to handle. Experimental evidence has shown that effective counseling can be carried on utilizing the computer. Obviously, cases do arise for which the computer has not been programed, and in such instances the computer would direct the student to seek the help of a counselor.

There are two basic approaches for utilizing the computer for instruction. The first is Computer-Managed Instruction (CMI) which utilizes the computer for recording biographical and performance data on students as well as prescribing student learning activities. The computer in this situation is programed to analyze student data and suggest learning activities which will result in the greatest amount of achievement for the student. The computer when used in this fashion does not necessarily have any responsibility for actually carrying out instruction, but assists the teacher in managing an individualized program of instruction which mainly relies on conventional materials.

The second instructional mode of operation of the computer is called

Computer-Assisted Instruction (CAI). Richard C. Atkinson, a leader in the field of CAI, has delineated three levels of sophistication of operation in this mode. These levels are called drill and practice, tutorial, and dialogue.

The drill and practice mode of operation is one in which the computer drills students on material which has been taught earlier by some conventional means. It is analagous to the flash cards used to drill children in elementary school on arithmetic problems. However, every problem is presented to each individual student, and these problems can be selected by the computer to fit the level of difficulty which is appropriate.

The tutorial mode of operation is different from drill and practice in that it actually takes the responsibility for the teaching of new material. This is accomplished through the use of techniques such as programed instruction, which was mentioned earlier in this section. Naturally, when the computer is used instead of regularly printed materials a great deal more flexibility is possible. It should also be mentioned that this mode of operation represents the most sophisticated instructional use of the computer so far achieved.

Atkinson anticipates that there is a level beyond tutorial CAI which he calls dialogue. Simply speaking, this mode would be one in which the computer would be able to understand spoken language and would be able to reply by speaking in order that an actual conversation could be carried on between the computer and the student. While many technical problems are still unresolved, research has developed computers which are capable of understanding certain words and phrases and can reply by playing back prerecorded messages or series of messages.

As time goes on it seems as if we can expect ever increasing use of computers in an educational setting. Computer costs are rapidly going down, and at the moment, the only great limitation is the development of materials for the computer to use for instruction. This is really a human limitation involving the training of teachers to write these materials and to devise creative ways in which the computer can be used.

A systems approach to teaching

Like most newcomers to a subject, students in education seek answers—immediate answers—to all of the problems that the teacher must face. While this is only natural, they soon discover that the instructor doesn't have the answers, and he questions whether there are any final answers. At such an apparent lack of intelligence, especially since most subject matter professors do have the answers, some students become frustrated, hyper-critical, and negative about professional education. The most difficult concept for the beginning education student to grasp is that in teaching there are no cut and dried final answers; each situation is unique, and what works one time may possibly be a dismal failure the next. And so the education instructor has no patented "cookbook" that he can hand out to students that will give them just the right answer at the right time. Of course there are principles, suggestions, and ideas that might work, but the student must seek out the answers himself in terms of his specific situation. This is the purpose of this small book—not as a panacea, but perhaps there might be some right answers for you. Students in education are first and foremost concerned with survival techniques: How can I survive as a student teacher? How can I survive on my first teaching job? An interesting paperback book which may be helpful is *The Teacher's Survival Guide* by Jenny Gray (Fearon Publishers).

Most students have a pretty good general idea of what a teacher has to do. However, when the student faces his first teaching assignment, he must think of the specific tasks to be performed. The specific question becomes, "What do I do now?" The simple answer might be—*start teaching!* However, many cannot even define teaching—"All you gotta do is tell 'em." Here is a helpful definition: "To teach is to motivate, to stimulate, to organize the materials in a meaningful way, and to make possible the conditions of learning."

Too many teachers think in terms of "what do *I* have to do?". Educational technology puts the shoe on the other foot and asks, "What do *students* have to do to achieve the objectives or competencies involved in the lesson, unit, or course?" To organize the curriculum in such a way that optimum learning can take place, educators have come up with what they call the "systems" approach. This is a procedure used successfully by business and industry to maximize production and efficiency. While the situation in education differs greatly, the approach utilizes all of the resources of educational technology.

The systems approach views the entire educational program as a system of closely interrelated parts. It is an orchestrated learning pattern with all parts harmoniously integrated into the whole: the school, the teacher, the students, the media, and the materials. Such an approach integrates the older, more familiar methods and tools of instruction with the new ones—the computer, television, programed instruction, and simulations, to name a few.

While much of this sounds highly esoteric and beyond the thinking of the beginning teacher, it places the role of the teacher and the answer to "What do I have to do?" in an entirely different perspective. The elements, while simple in theory, are often difficult in practice, but they may represent much of the educational practice of the future. To begin with, teachers and curriculum planners must determine as accurately as possible the desired terminal outcomes of instruction—the exit behavior. This is often referred to as "task analysis" and is our old buddy—instructional objectives.

Next to be considered is the "entry behavior" of the individual student—his knowledge, attitudes, and learning skills. After this the various resources should be taken into account—people and materials available to provide those experiences which may enable the student to achieve the desired learning outcomes. An attempt must then be made to determine experimentally the most effective sequences of these learning experiences and the varied media used in developing them. Also, some techniques for evaluating the learning outcomes must be included. However, only after numerous trials and modifications is the system ready for operation.

Sounds pretty complicated doesn't it? However, in a sense, most effective teachers use such an approach. While the teacher methodology may be somewhat haphazard and unscientific, through trial and error students may reach the desirable learning outcomes. However, this may be achieved with considerable pain and suffering, loss of time and effort, and may create a distinct dislike for the subject.

The development of a course utilizing a learning-systems concept includes exactly the same steps as the programed learning approach. In other words, programed instruction is simply one example of a systems approach. A program consists of a carefully planned sequence of items which leads to a level of competency for a specified subject. The higher level systems approach attempts, through task analysis and program planning, to marshall all of the instructional resources available in order to maximize the learning situation. On the other hand, programed instruction normally uses a single medium—a self-instructional programed text.

Therefore, it would appear that educational planners (which should include teachers) might look to the systems approach in planning the total curriculum of a school. Within this totality, the subject matter departments can develop their "systems" which can then be broken down for the individual classrooms using a multi-media programed approach.

Teaching for mastery

Technology is advancing at a tremendous pace and is providing the teacher with tools to do jobs never before considered possible. The arsenal of procedures available is indeed impressive, but the task of incorporating these new developments in the schools to the best advantage is the subject of continual evaluation.

Technology is one thing, but what do we know about the student? Specifically, what do we know about his learning characteristics? A long list of sources might be quoted to substantiate the veracity of each of the following four variables. However, they are all things any teacher would say are common knowledge.

First, students vary widely in their aptitudes for particular kinds of learning. At one end of a continuum are students with a very special talent and at the opposite end are students with little or no talent in that subject area. In between these extremes are the 90 per cent or so of the students who are distributed over the remainder of the normal curve. One notion pertaining to this 90 per cent is that aptitude may be thought of as the amount of time required by the learner to attain mastery of a learning task. The implication here is that for the vast majority of students, mastery of a subject can be achieved if only the required amount of time that person needs can be allotted. If this premise is correct, it may be a poor policy and an unjust procedure to rigidly adhere to the practice of asking students to have learned a particular block of material in a fixed time, such as, a term or semester.

Second, some students respond to one method of instruction better than another. For example, a student might do well working on his own using programed materials, but not do well in a standard lecture section. It is to be emphasized here that we are talking about individuals and not groups. Methods of instruction as a general rule do not differ greatly in their effectiveness when groups are compared, but it may make tremendous differences to particular individuals.

A third variable pertaining to student learning characteristics is the ability to understand instruction. Considering procedures normally used in schools at present, this factor would be determined by verbal ability and reading comprehension. It is believed that the biggest changes in the amount of learning a student could achieve would result from employing different teaching procedures which do not rely greatly on this type of ability. That is, a student who is not doing well because of poor verbal ability might do better if group study, tutorial help, programed instruction, or audiovisual materials were used.

Fourth, students vary in the amount of perseverance they bring to the learning task. Perseverance in this context is to be thought of as the amount of time the learner is willing to spend in learning. This factor may be related to frustration or anxiety level. Rather than giving training in the development of better perseverance, it is undoubtedly easier and probably more effective to demand less perseverance of students. Research indicates that demands for perseverance may be sharply reduced if students are provided with instructional resources most appropriate for them. Since the emphasis in education should be on learning, there seems little virtue in making learning difficult for the vague and perhaps ill-conceived notion of discipline and endurance.

So far in this discussion, four aspects of individual differences in learners have been reviewed. Each one makes a great difference in how any particular individual will succeed in school, and yet two practices prevail in education which seem almost ludicrous in light of this discussion. First, the time allotted to learn something is the same for each student. Definite time periods are fixed for every learning task, and all students must learn the material within that allotted time or suffer the consequences. Second, the consequences arrive disguised as the "normal" curve. Insult is added to injury by evaluating the individual student with what is known about the group. The emphasis in testing becomes achieving a range of well distributed scores rather than evaluating each student against a fixed set of criteria to discover whether he has learned what we desire of him.

It is one thing to be critical of current practices, but what techniques are at our disposal to correct the ills and do a better job? Are there alternatives to the present mode of teaching which might allow us to teach every student to a level of mastery?

A precondition to this type of teaching involves the specification of the behavioral objectives which the instruction will be designed to accomplish. These objectives must *all* be strictly stated in terms of *exactly* what is to be observed, under what conditions it will be observed, and what the standard of performance will be. An excellent guide in this process is *Preparing Instructional Objectives* by Robert F. Mager. This rather short book is written as a branching programed book and deals with the subject in a superb fashion. The reader is referred to this work for a discussion of the preparation of good instructional objectives. For purposes here, it is sufficient to say that these objectives must be stated in such a fashion that they describe the act the learner must perform to demonstrate that he acquired the knowledge or skill required of him.

When objectives are prepared in this manner, it becomes a simple matter to evaluate students on the basis of their accomplishment of the minimum acceptable criteria embodied in the objectives. In this situation students are evaluated against a set of established explicit criteria or objectives which they have been informed about. At present in education, we often make a big secret of what it is we want students to learn. Nothing can be more ridiculous; if one wants a student to learn something, why not tell him what it is? Through the use of objectives, the student is informed of exactly what it is he has to learn and exactly the manner in which he will achieve these objectives and be evaluated for the accomplishment of said objectives.

It should be pointed out here that so far the discussion has referred to evaluation and *not* grades. In this proposal, grades are seen to be irrelevant to the teaching process. Students should simply be evaluated to see if they have accomplished the stated objectives of the course of instruction. If they have, then they should go ahead to new material; if not, then further instruction should be prescribed until such time as they are able to satisfactorily meet the objectives. In this way, failure is eliminated.

At this point it may be well to take a break from these more theoretical considerations and outline a specific example of the implementation of such a program. Let us, for example, consider courses such as English or basic mathematics.

The first job for the instructor is to completely specify exactly what behaviors are desired of the students throughout the period of instruction. To account for the varying learning rates of the students, there would be no fixed length of time in which a student must learn the material. The only stipulation would be that a student could not take more advanced work in that subject area until he had demonstrated accomplishment of the course objectives.

To account for differences in individuals due to the method of instruction, some flexible arrangement might be made. One such procedure might be to use programed materials. This would not interfere with varying learning rates and would also be adaptable to any sort of special purpose during the course of study. For example, if a student needed additional reading materials, they could be added whenever he was ready for them. Naturally, this sort of flexibility would also take care of the third individual learning difference mentioned, i.e., the ability to understand instruction. Differences in verbal ability and reading comprehension, or mathematical and spatial reasoning, could be taken into account to prescribe the optimum method of instruction for each student.

Since the time allowed to complete instruction is open-ended, the factor of perseverance is taken into consideration. The learner would be allowed to spend whatever amount of time he was willing to devote. It is expected that with an open-ended time factor there would be some students who would meet the objectives at criterion level much earlier than under conventional organizations, and others who would take a great deal longer. The length of time they use, however, is not the important point. What is important is that *all* students completing the course will eventually perform at whatever level of competence you established.

Each student has his own particular problems and can benefit greatly from individual work prescribed for his particular case. A program such as this one would give him that opportunity. An experiment concerning this approach was conducted by the writer and is reported in *The Mathematics Teacher,* November 1967.

Throughout this discussion it has been either implied, or directly stated, that students ought to be treated differently in harmony with their individual differences. How is this prescription for study arrived at? What are the bases for choosing the type of treatment a student will get? This problem has not as yet been solved, but a good start has been made. There are strong indications that the ability of the student to understand instruction is closely related to his verbal ability and reading comprehension. Perseverance, it is believed, could be related to the student's anxiety level or degree of frustration. Moreover, there are indications that the method of instruction may relate to neuroticism or extroversion scales. All of these are only indications which could result in fruitful research. However, at present the teacher is still "playing his best hunch" on the prescriptions he makes. Playing hunches still seems preferable, however, to the traditional procedure of prescribing the same treatment for all students.

Technology has come a long way in giving teachers better tools with which to ply their trade. It has always been recognized that people are different from each other and need to be treated differently in the classroom; however, with heavy class loads and many sections to teach, individualization has become a near impossibility using conventional practices. It seems increasingly imperative that these old practices be partially set aside in favor of the various technological boosts that are available. It is time for educators to think in terms of a multi-media approach to teaching and capitalizing on the particular abilities manifested in each individual. In education we have no immediately measurable product, but we provide a service. The only real measure of the effectiveness of that service is an assessment of the intellectual and emotional growth of our students. There are many new tools available to help do a greatly improved job. Let's not let the tools sit idle in our arsenal when the means are at hand to put them to work.

More on technology

Atkinson, Richard C. and Wilson, H. A., eds. *Computer-Assisted Instruction: A Book of Readings.* New York: Academic Press Inc., 1969.

Block, James H. ed., *Mastery Learning: Theory and Practice.* New York: Holt, Rinehart and Winston, 1971.

Bloom, Benjamin S. *Learning For Mastery.* The Regional Education Laboratory for the Carolinas and Virginia (RELCV). Topical Papers and Reprints No. 1.

Hickey, Albert E., ed. *Computer-Assisted Instruction: A Survey of the Literature.* ENTELEK Inc., 1968.

Loughary, John W., *Man-Machine Systems in Education.* New York: Harper and Row, 1966.

Lysaught, Jerome P. and Williams, Clarence M. *A Guide to Programmed Instruction.* New York: John Wiley and Sons, Inc., 1963.

Mager, Robert F. *Preparing Instructional Objectives.* Palo Alto, Calif.; Fearon Publishers, 1962.

Markle, Susan M., Eigen, Lewis D. and Komoski, Kenneth. *A Programmed Primer on Programing.* The Center for Programed Instruction, 1961.

Popham, W. James and Baker, Eva L. *Establishing Instructional Goals.* Englewood Cliffs, N.J.: Prentice-Hall Inc., 1970.

———. *Planning an Instructional Sequence.* Englewood Cliffs, N.J.: Prentice-Hall Inc., 1970.

———. *Systematic Instruction.* Englewood Cliffs, N.J.: Prentice-Hall Inc., 1970.

Skinner, B. F. *The Technology of Teaching.* New York: Appleton-Century-Crofts, 1968.

PART 3

Just Plain Laboratory Practice

What do I have to do?

First of all, you can do something or you can do nothing. If you choose the latter, how in the world did you get this far? If you choose to do something, then BE NOT AFRAID! The machines are perfectly safe; there is nothing to fear; they won't run away from you; they won't climb a tree; they won't hurt you (men—be careful of those wide ties—I once threaded mine through a motion picture projector). You won't damage the machines (unless you drop them on the floor!); you can't plug them in wrong; you can't hurt them by turning on the wrong switch; BUT . . . you can damage materials—and they cost dough—use practice materials to practice.

For a limited competency in the operation of equipment, students ought to be able to pass a *performance check out* on the following:

1. Filmstrip and slide projector
2. Tape recorder
3. Two different models of motion picture projectors

To develop a higher level of competency, students may wish to practice on the following:

1. Other makes and models of filmstrip-slide projectors, tape recorders, and motion picture projectors
2. Other types of equipment including the overhead and opaque projectors, the dry-mounting press, and the spirit duplicator

Laboratory practice will vary according to the professional program. Some institutions may have rigidly scheduled time-blocks, specific minimum practice hours, and a stiff check-out exam. On the other hand, some programs may be on an entirely voluntary basis; the sole responsibility for competency rests with the individual student (ideally, exactly where it ought to be). However, somewhere in the middle of the two extremes appears as a more practical approach.

With most of the equipment in the media laboratory, some general operating principles can be applied. While the specifics of operation may vary with the make, type, and model of machine, these general principles can be a valuable aid to the teacher confronted with a totally unfamiliar machine. Usually, the specifics for operation will come with the machine or are contained somewhere on the chassis or case.

In the following sections, general operating principles for the film-strip-slide projector, tape recorder, and motion picture projector are presented.

Competency: filmstrip—slide projector

A. Objectives and Evaluation

Students should be able to set up projector, thread filmstrip and insert slides properly, and effectively project these materials.

Evaluation of your competency ought to be based upon *performance* with a three- to five-minute time limit for each of the materials involved.

B. Filmstrip Projection

1. *Set-up*
   a. Open the lid and remove projector from case. The projector *must not* be used in the case. Air must flow freely beneath the machine in order for the fan to cool the projection lamp. (In some instances, air louvres are built into the case, then the projector remains in the case.)
   b. Unwind the power cord and place plug into wall receptacle. When you finish *always* remove cord from wall by the *plug*.

2. *The filmstrip adaptor*
   a. Locate the knurled bolt attached to the lens barrel. This bolt should be facing toward the ceiling, if not, turn lens barrel so that it is.
   b. Take the *filmstrip adaptor* (it's that funny looking thing with the red knob and windows in it) and insert it into the slot provided behind the lens barrel. There is only one way it can go in. You may have to jiggle it a little or adjust the knurled bolt, but don't force it.
      1. Make sure it is inserted all the way so that lens barrel can be turned.

2. Tighten knurled bolt and rotate lens barrel so that knurled
   bolt is on right side and red knob is towards bottom.

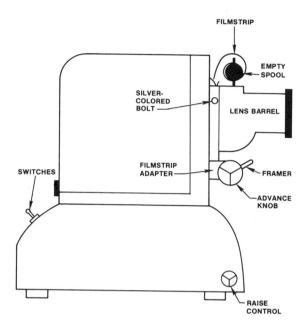

Filmstrip Projector

3. *Focus and tilt controls*
   a. The projector is focused by rotating the lens (that round black
      thing on the end). The closer the screen, the more the lens
      must be rotated out.
   b. To raise or lower the projector, turn the tilt or elevator knob
      located on the lower right-hand corner of the projector.
   c. Pre-focus—it is difficult to pre-focus for slides of filmstrips until
      after they have been inserted into the projector. However, by
      turning on the motor and lamp switch (located at the rear
      of the projector) you may make some adjustments as to projec-
      tor height and the direction of the light to the screen. If possible,
      all of the above should be completed before the class assembles.

4. *Threading the filmstrip.* In order not to damage the filmstrip,
   extreme care must be exercised in handling it.
   a. Remove the filmstrip from its container by carefully inserting
      your finger and rotating the finger as you pull film out of
      the container toward you.

    b. The filmstrip is inserted into the projector *upside down.* To position the filmstrip, face the screen, hold the strip up so that you can read the printing and the pictures are right side up. Now rotate the filmstrip 180 degrees so that it is upside down and the printing is backwards. It is now ready to insert into the filmstrip carrier.

    c. Hold the film along the edges and gently push the end between the two glass plates (film channel) of the filmstrip adaptor until it stops. Then slowly turn the red knob in counter-clockwise direction (feeding film at same time) until the film comes out bottom of adaptor.

5. *Showing the filmstrip*
   a. Turn on the motor and lamp switch and focus image on the screen by rotating lens.
   b. If a part of two frames appears on the screen, this may be corrected by moving the framing lever up or down. Correct so that each movement of the advance knob moves the filmstrip one whole frame.
   c. If the screen image is not level, the lens barrel may have to be turned and the projector leveled.
   d. Rotate the advance knob until it reaches the title frame and you're ready to go!

6. *Finishing up*
   a. Upon reaching the caption "The End" turn off the lamp switch and continue turning the advance knob until you can remove the filmstrip from the projector.
   b. To return the filmstrip to its container, it must be rolled up tightly. Start with "The End" of the filmstrip and form a loop about the size of a pencil. Then roll carefully by holding it along the edges. *Do not pull* on the filmstrip—this will put scratches on the film.

C. Slide Projection (sometimes called 2 x 2 slides or 35 mm.)

1. *Set-up* (Directions are the same as 1a and 1b in the filmstrip section).

2. *The slide adaptor*
   a. If the filmstrip adaptor is still in the projector, turn the lens barrel so that the knurled bolt is toward the ceiling. Loosen the bolt and remove the filmstrip adaptor.
   b. Insert slide adaptor (holder) into the slot formerly occupied

by the filmstrip adaptor and push it in as far as it will go. Tighten the knurled bolt.

c. Note the little black or red plastic attachment on top that moves. This is the handle for sliding slides.

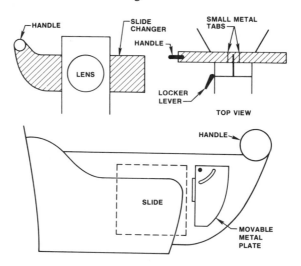

Slide Projector, Slide Carrier

3. *Inserting the slides*

   a. Move the handle of the slide holder to one extreme position, either right or left.

   b. A slide is positioned in exactly the same manner in which you positioned the filmstrip. Review paragraph *B-4-a* in the preceding section and then perform the same operation with the slide; then insert it into the open slot of the carrier.

   c. Pull (or push) the slide carrier to the other extreme. The slide is now in the aperture for projection, and the carrier in position to insert another slide. With the second slide, repeat "b" above and insert into the open slot of the carrier. Pull or push second slide to aperture position.

   d. Turn on the lamp switch and motor, then focus and level the machine.

   e. To insert a new slide, remove the slide in the carrier slot; now open and follow procedures listed above. *Always* turn off lamp before removing last slide.

   f. Note that as you moved the handle of the slide holder a space appeared on the opposite end of the holder to insert another slide. Insert second slide (upside down and backwards) into this slot, pull handle of slide holder toward you and slide two will appear on screen. Remove slide one and insert slide three, and so on, etc.

D. Some Brownie Points

1. At the end of a showing, it is possible to increase the life of the projection lamp by turning off the lamp switch and permitting the motor to run to cool off the lamp.
   Important—since discussion must take place immediately after a showing, the motor noise may interfere with the discussion—then turn it off!

2. If you have to change a bulb, cool the bulb before handling. Remove the bulb by pressing down while turning counter-clockwise. The flanges of the new bulb must be lined up with the slots in the socket as it is pressed down and rotated clockwise.

3. If the lens, glass plates of the filmstrip holder, and reflectors are kept clean, you will get a better picture. This is done with *lens* tissue, and the lab assistant will gladly show you how.

Slides and filmstrips are great teaching tools—you control them—set the pace—can individualize—and *you* are the sound track!

Competency: motion picture projector

A. Objectives and Evaluation

Students should be able to set up projector, thread the film properly, effectively project the film along with adequate sound track level, and rewind the film.

Evaluation of your competency ought to be based upon *performance* with a 5- to 7-minute time limit for the entire operation—not including rewind and take-down.

B. Basic Operating Principles

Certain basic principles apply to all motion picture projectors. A thorough understanding of these principles should enable you to grasp easily the specific operating directions for each machine (threading diagrams are usually included on the chassis or case of the projector). If the projector is the self-threading or cartridge type, then you must follow the specific instructions that come with the machine.

1. Threading a projector is like driving a car; all cars and all projectors are different, but the operating principles are the same. It goes like this:
   a. Over sprocket wheel #1.
   b. Make upper loop (usually an outline on the chassis, no smaller, no larger than the width of two fingers.
   c. Open film gate, insert film, close tightly.
   d. Make lower loop (two fingers in width).
   e. Pass film tightly over sound drum and onto sprocket wheel #2.
   f. Insert film onto take-up reel.

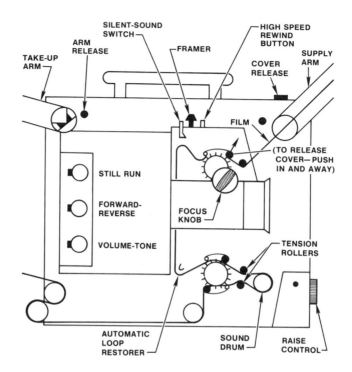

Motion Picture Projector

C. Helpful Hints—Some Checks and Double Checks:

   1. Always check the projector before threading (On forward? Sound speed? Amp. working? Exciter lamp on? Pre-focus?)

   2. Always double-check your threading (sprocket holes engaged? Loops right? Film tight over sound drum?).

   3. Research has firmly established that, if possible, the mechanics of projection *should not* interfere with the instructional nature of the presentation. Therefore, it is essential to provide a *smooth* showing by *checking the projector,* double-*checking* your threading and following these steps to start:
      a. Sound on, but down.
      b. Turn on motor switch (make sure film is moving through projector properly).
      c. Turn on the projection lamp.
      d. Adjust focus and framing.

  e. Sound slowly up.

4. Finish up by turning the:
  a. Sound down.
  b. Lamp off.
  c. Motor off.

5. Just a little more:
  a. If the film has been rewound properly when you begin to thread it, the sprocket holes (the little square things with nothing inside) should be facing you.
  b. The film will *then* come off the *feed-reel* clockwise and be placed on the *take-up reel* in the *same* direction.
  c. *Do* pre-focus, center, and level the projector, if possible.
     Do start the film (that is, throw on the lamp switch) upon the opening title.
     Do have the volume down or you'll knock the kids out of their seats.
     Do turn the sound down and the lamp off when "The End" gets there.
     Do give the film a chance—it is a great teaching tool—but it is more abused than used properly!

D. Rewind

1. The rewind operation can be simple or complex, depending on the machine.

2. In most class situations, *do not rewind* the film unless you or another teacher are to use the film again. When the film is returned to the Instructional Media Center, it will be rewound and inspected at the same time.

3. If there is anything wrong with the film, insert a note for the inspector in the film can. If the film breaks, put the broken end of the film (you may have to rethread) under the broken end on the take-up reel. Turn the reel, one full turn to grasp the film coming from the projector. *Do not use* paper clips, glue, scotch tape, or bubble gum!

Competency: tape recorder

A. Objectives and Evaluation

Students should be able to set up a tape recorder, thread the tape, record, playback, rewind, and use the recorder as a public address system.

Evaluation of your competency ought to be based upon *performance* with 4- to 6-minutes for the entire operation.

B. Basic Operating Principles

Similar to the motion picture projector, there are certain basic operating principles for *all* tape recorders, it is useless to *memorize* the operation of one machine. Therefore, an understanding of the basic principles should enable you to grasp the specific operating instructions for each machine.

1. The analogy of driving a car and threading a motion picture projector also applies to operating a tape recorder—know the basic principles.

2. The five basic operations of the tape recorder are: threading; playback; recording; rewind; and using it as a public address system.
   a. Threading
      1. Place the full reel of tape on the left-hand spindle and the empty reel on the right-hand spindle.
      2. Hold a section of tape, with the shiny side toward you, taut between the fingers of both hands and insert into the slot next to the recording head (the dull side of the tape must be next to the head—this is the recording or working side).

3. Insert the tape into the slot of the empty reel; turn at least one turn and make sure tape is secure.

b. Playback
1. To "play" a tape, the amplifier is turned on and the machine placed in the "play" position by either pushing a button or turning a knob.
2. To play back a tape after a recording, you must rewind the tape.
3. However, it is important to know that most classroom tape recorders either play back or record on only one-half the width of the tape. Therefore, when all of the tape from the supply reel has passed through the machine, the right reel (now the full reel) is turned over, placed on the left spindle, and the empty reel placed on the right spindle. Now you can start all over again.

c. Recording
1. Turn amplifier switch to "on" (usually this is the volume control).
2. Plug the microphone into the microphone input jack (check to see that monitor switch is off).
3. Pre-set the volume by pressing the "record button" (do not start the reel moving). Speak slowly into the microphone and adjust the volume until the recording volume is correct. This is indicated when the "eye" (or whatever indicator is used) is barely moving.
4. To record, it usually takes *two* operations. (Since the machine erases and records at the same time, this prevents the operator from inadvertently erasing the tape.) By either pushing two buttons, turning one knob and pushing one button, or turning two knobs, the machine is placed in "record" position.
5. To record merely speak into the microphone (about six inches away from mouth).
6. Note the recording level indicator (may be an eye, meter, or bulb); this is a device to help the operator adjust the volume for the best recording level. It will indicate whether the volume is too high, too low, or just right.
7. If the recorder has a footage meter—note the numbers when you started to record. This facilitates rewinding in order to return to the place where you started to record.

d. Rewind
1. To rewind the tape, push a button or turn a knob to place

the machine in rewind position and let'er rip. (Note that sometimes there is a fast rewind and also a forward or fast forward position—experiment with these.)

   e. Using the tape recorder as a public address system

      1. Sometimes it is helpful to know that you can amplify your voice by using the tape recorder as a public address system (you can also use a motion picture projector for the same purpose).

      2. You will note that each tape recorder usually has what is called a "monitor." By turning the monitor switch to "on," it is possible to listen to what you are actually recording onto the tape.

      3. On most tape recorders, by plugging in the microphone, turning on the amplifier switch and the monitor switch, and placing the machine in "record" position (not necessary to thread a tape) the tape recorder now becomes a public address system. *Warning:* Any time the monitor switch is on, be careful of *feedback*. This high squeal is caused by the volume being too high and the mike too close to the recorder.

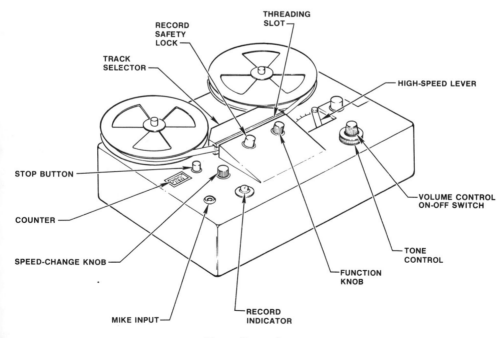

Tape Recorder

PART 4
Resources

Resources

A. In the Media Lab

   1. Production: While facilities for production may be limited by the
      size of the lab and the program, most lab instructors will attempt
      to help students in many ways. Ask for help with:
      a. Making transparencies
      b. Dry mounting of pictures
      c. Copying materials on the opaque projector for study displays
      d. Running off dittos (you supply the paper)

   2. How-to-do-it handouts: Some labs have compiled a list and in-
      structions of useful "how-to-do-it" projects for teachers—ask about
      them.

   3. Books, catalogs, and manuals: Most labs will have a collection
      of media textbooks, audio-visual catalogs, and equipment and
      production manuals. Browse through these; they contain many
      valuable classroom ideas.

B. Other Sources

   1. Media textbooks
      a. Brown, J. W.; Lewis, R. B., and Harcleroad, F. F. *A. V. Instruc-
         tion: Media and Methods.* New York: McGraw-Hill Book Co.,
         3rd ed., 1969.
      b. Dale, Edgar. *Audiovisual Methods In Teaching.* New York: Holt,
         Rinehart and Winston, 3rd ed., 1969.
      c. Kinder, J. S. *Audio-Visual Materials and Techniques.* New York:
         American Book Co., 2nd ed., 1959.
      d. Wittich, W. A., and Schuler, C. F. *Audio-Visual Materials.* New
         York: Harper and Row, 4th ed., 1967.

2. Laboratory Manuals
   a. Eboch, S. C. *Operating Audiovisual Equipment.* San Francisco: Chandler Publishing Co., 2nd ed., 1968.
   b. Davidson, R. L. *Audiovisual Machines.* New York: Intn'l Textbook Co., 1969.
   c. Minor, E., and Frye, H. R. *Techniques for Producing Visual Instructional Media.* New York: McGraw-Hill Book Co., 1970.
   d. Nelson, L. W. *Instructional Aids.* Dubuque, Iowa: Wm. C. Brown Co., 1970.
   e. Oates, S. C. *Audio-Visual Equipment, Self-Instruction Manual.* Dubuque, Iowa: Wm. C. Brown Co., 1966.
   f. Sally, H. E., et al. *Equipment Operation Manual.* Dubuque, Iowa: Wm. C. Brown Co., 1968.
   g. Wyman, R. *Media Ware.* Dubuque, Iowa: Wm. C. Brown Co., 1969.

3. Miscellaneous
   a. Aubrey, R. H. *Selected Free Materials.* Palo Alto, Calif.: Fearon Publishers, 1967.
   b. *Bridges for Ideas,* Professional Handbook Series (Paper, $2.50 ea), 1970.
      Basic Design and Utilization of Instructional T.V.
      Instructional Display Boards
      The Overhead System
      Local Production Techniques
      Production of 2 x 2 Slides
      Educational Displays and Exhibits
      The Tape Recorder
      Better Bulletin Boards
      Models for Teaching
      Using Tear Sheets

      All available from Instructional Media Center, Univ. of Texas at Austin, Drawer W., University Station, Austin, Texas 78712.
   c. Educators Guide Series, *Free Films, Free Filmstrips.* Randolph, Wisconsin: Educators Progress Service, Inc., 1970.
   d. Kemp, J. E. *Planning and Producing Audiovisual Materials.* San Francisco: Chandler Publishing Co., 2nd ed., 1968.
   f. Scuorzo, H. E. *Practical Audio-Visual Handbook for Teachers.* West Nyack, N.Y.: Parker Pub. Co., 1967.
   g. U. S. Government Printing Office, Superintendent of Documents, Washington, D.C., 20402 (Free booklets, pamphlets).

h. Williams, C. M. "Learning From Pictures," 2nd ed., N.E.A., Washington, D.C., 1968.

4. Media Periodicals
   a. *Audiovisual Instruction.* Dept. of Audiovisual Instruction, N.E.A., 1201 Sixteenth St. N.W., Washington, D.C. 20036
   b. *AV Communication Review* (research). Dept. of Audiovisual Instruction, N.E.A., 1201 Sixteenth St. N.W., Washington, D.C. 20036
   c. *Education Age.* 3M Education Press, St. Paul, Minn. 55101
   d. *Educational Screen and AV Guide.* 434 S. Wabash, Chicago, Ill. 60605
   e. *Educational Technology.* 456 Sylvan Ave., Englewood Cliffs, N.J. 07632
   f. *Educational Television.* 140 Main St., Richfield, Conn. 06877
   g. *Media and Methods.* 134 N. 13th St., Philadelphia, Pa. 19107
   h. *NSPI Journal.* National Society for Programmed Instruction, 715 Stadium Dr., San Antonio, Texas 78212

5. Media and "How To Do It" films

Accent on Learning	B/W, 30 mins
Audio-Visual Aids to Learning	B/W, 10 mins
Better Bulletin Boards	Color, 13 mins
Bringing the World to the Classroom	B/W, 22 mins
Bulletin Boards: An Effective Teaching Device	Color, 10 mins
Chalk and Chalkboards	Color, 15 mins
Chalk Board Utilization	B/W, 15 mins
Charts for Creative Learning	Color, 10 mins
Children Learn From Filmstrips	Color, 17 mins
Communications Revolution	B/W, 22 mins
Dry Mount Your Teaching Pictures	B/W, 10 mins
Duplicating By the Spirit Method	Color, 15 mins
Effective Listening	B/W, 15 mins
Feltboard in Teaching	Color, 10 mins
Film and You: Using the Classroom Film	Color, 13 mins
Film Tactics	B/W, 22 mins
Flannel Boards and How to Use Them	Color, 15 mins
Flannelgraph	Color, 30 mins
Globes: Their Function in the Classroom	Color, 14 mins
Handmade Materials for Projection	Color, 20 mins
How to Make a Mask	Color, 10 mins
How to Make a Puppet	Color, 10 mins
How to Make and Use a Diorama	Color, 20 mins

How to Make Hand Made Lantern Slides	Color, 21 mins
How to Teach With Films	B/W, 16 mins
How to Use a Class Film	Color, 17 mins
Instructional Film: New Way to Greater Ed.	B/W, 15 mins
Learning and Behavior (Teaching Machine)	B/W, 26 mins
Lettering Instructional Materials	Color, 20 mins
Magazines to Transparencies	Color, 12 mins
Magnetic Tape Recording	B/W, 8 mins
Make a Movie Without a Camera	Color, 6 mins
Make a Mobile	Color, 11 mins
Making Films That Teach	B/W, 20 mins
Mimeographing Techniques	Color, 17 mins
Opaque Projector, Part 2, Utilization	B/W, 10 mins
Overhead Projector	B/W, 16 mins
Photographic Slides for Instruction	Color, 11 mins
Preparing Projected Materials	Color, 15 mins
Projecting Ideas on the Overhead Projector	Color, 17 mins
Second Classroom, The	B/W, 30 mins
Sight and Sound	B/W, 11 mins
Tape Recording for Instruction	B/W, 15 mins
Teacher and Technology	B/W, 59 mins
Television System	B/W, 15 mins
Television Techniques for Teachers	Color, 25 mins
This Is Marshall McLuhan: Part I	Color, 24 mins
Part II	Color, 29 mins
Time-Lapse Photography	Color, 10 mins
Unique Contribution (Educ. Films)	Color, 29 mins
Using the Classroom Film	B/W, 22 mins
Using Visual Aids in Training	B/W, 14 mins
Using Visuals in Your Speech	B/W, 15 mins
Wet Mounting Pictorial Materials	Color, 10 mins
What Are Teaching Machines?	B/W, 30 mins
Your Movie Camera and How to Use It	B/W, 10 mins